# The Recovery of
# Love

Text copyright © Naomi Starkey 2012
The author asserts the moral right
to be identified as the author of this work

**Published by**
**The Bible Reading Fellowship**
15 The Chambers, Vineyard
Abingdon OX14 3FE
United Kingdom
Tel: +44 (0)1865 319700
Email: enquiries@brf.org.uk
Website: www.brf.org.uk
BRF is a Registered Charity

ISBN 978 1 84101 892 8
First published 2012
10 9 8 7 6 5 4 3 2 1 0
All rights reserved

**Acknowledgments**
Unless otherwise stated, scripture quotations are taken from the New Revised Standard
Version of the Bible, Anglicised edition, copyright © 1989, 1995 by the Division of Christian
Education of the National Council of the Churches of Christ in the United States of America,
and are used by permission. All rights reserved.

Scripture quotations taken from the Holy Bible, New International Version, copyright © 1973,
1978, 1984 by Biblica (formerly International Bible Society), are used by permission of Hodder
& Stoughton Publishers, a member of the Hachette Livre Group UK. All rights reserved. 'NIV'
is a registered trademark of Biblica. UK trademark number 1448790.

The paper used in the production of this publication was supplied by mills that source their
raw materials from sustainably managed forests. Soy-based inks were used in its printing and
the laminate film is biodegradable.

A catalogue record for this book is available from the British Library

Printed in Singapore by Craft Print International Ltd

# The Recovery of

# Love

WALKING THE WAY OF WHOLENESS

# Naomi Starkey

*'Our purpose is love: to be loved, to love,*
*and to spread God's love.'*
Rachel Boulding

To the staff of BRF, past and present,
who have been not only colleagues but
companions on my own journey

## Acknowledgments

*Thanks to the Great Oak Cafe, Llanidloes*
*(and their root ginger cake with lemon icing),*
*where a significant part of this book was written.*

*Particular thanks to those kind people who read through*
*the work-in-progress and offered suggestions and encouragement:*
*Gilly, Lisa, Richard, Andy, Andrew, Kristina and Mike.*

# Contents

# Introduction

Some people like to be taken on mystery tours; others prefer to have a clear idea of where they are going, and why, and how long it will take, and where they will stop for lunch. This book is, in some ways, a bit of a mystery tour, inspired in part by (although in no way claiming parity with) classic Christian dream texts such as *The Pilgrim's Progress*, *Piers Plowman* and *The Great Divorce*, and also by the whole rich tradition of storytelling as a way of exploring aspects of faith and truth.

It begins in a city, evoking the stress and demands endemic to life in today's busy, predominantly urban culture. It also ends in the same city, but this city now reverberates with a little of the imagery of the city of God, the new Jerusalem, which scripture promises us is our final home. In between, the narrative takes us to explore a curious yet safe place, a mysterious house of many rooms where questions can be asked, experiences shared and the search for healing begun.

Using story, reflection on Bible passages and quotations for further thought from a range of Christian writers, the trajectory of the book is from emptiness and despair to certain hope, from confusion through penitence to the great joy of forgiving and receiving forgiveness. A constant theme is the interplay between God's unmerited grace and mercy and our human failings; at the heart of the story is the meaning of love—on the one hand, our hunger for it and our often weary search to find and secure it, and on the other hand, God's breathtaking love for us, his children, expressed supremely in the birth, life, sacrificial death and resurrection of Jesus.

The good news that we have been given to share is that the world's hunger for love can be met only in God's never-ending embrace. Before that hunger can be understood, however, one question must be pondered and eventually answered: what do we really want?

What do you really want?

It is time to begin.

Part One

# In search of love

# 1
# Planet Babylon

Welcome to the city. It is morning.

Walk with me now, under the hazy blue of the morning city sky, along the choked arterial road as tourist coaches grind their way past, bringing load after load of budget travellers to sample the glittering opportunities of the metropolis. Everywhere we look, there is transport—the angry buzz of motorbikes, bumper-to-bumper cars (as the traffic lights change, take care that they don't run you down in their desperation to hurtle to the next junction), packed trains on the viaduct overhead, plane after plane skimming the tower blocks on their descent to the airport. It seems as if everybody is coming to the city.

'Where is this city?' you may ask. Well, perhaps you think you recognise something of the place where we walk, but it is both somewhere and nowhere. It is made of random memories of 21st-century urban landscapes but, at the same time, it is the big city of so many stories, where people come to chase their dreams, make their fortunes and shape for themselves a new life, even a new identity.

Many come to the city because they are young, bursting with their special blend of apparently inexhaustible energy and assumptions of invulnerability. For them, adult life is still shiny and new, and for most of them nothing much has gone wrong yet. They have come to work hard and play very, very hard, and few will spend time reflecting on the bleak expanses of old age that (they are pretty sure) begin on the morning of their 30th birthday. While many arrive young and leave young, others find a safe niche to live somewhere in the miles of streets, and one day discover to their surprise that they have stayed on into middle age and family life, perhaps even beyond that.

A great many, whatever their age, come to the city in the hope that here they will find love, whether expressed as temporary emotional thrill or physical release or that elusive true sweetheart, the man or woman of their most precious dreams. How could they not come across him or her, eventually, in such a huge tide of humanity? The beguiling anonymity of the city means that we can feel free to venture out in search of someone or something, confident that we will not bump into anybody from 'back home' who might remind us of the person we no longer want to be.

In the shops, the offices and the night clubs, in the pavement overspill from pubs and bars, on the dusty summer grass of the city parks, we come across people looking for connection, for some kind of love. A great many are fortunate, of course. One day they emerge hand in hand with another with whom they can build a home, which may mature over the years into a place of lifelong security and cherishing. For others, however, the connection remains unmade. Love stays elusive; the city's anonymity starts to oppress, to push them towards isolation, melancholy, fragmentation. There is nothing lonelier than walking through city streets, longing for consolation, for a way of making meaning from a hard turn of life events, but seeing nothing except the averted eyes of strangers.

The trouble, you see, is that the city may seduce us and promise much, but, at the end of the day, it does not particularly care. So much of its life is based around the making of money—and the human life of the city is shaped (you could say, warped) to fit the demands of that immense enterprise. Business generates wealth; leisure and culture generate wealth; crime generates significant amounts of wealth, and, of course, money itself generates enormous amounts of wealth. Love becomes no more than another commodity to be picked over, priced and traded at a substantial profit. Encompassing it all, the media (whether electronic or printed, spoken or written) is the mouth of the city, devouring everything for which it finds a taste and generating more wealth at the other end.

Then the angel carried me away in the Spirit into a desert. There I saw a woman sitting on a scarlet beast that was covered with blasphemous names and had seven heads and ten horns. The woman was dressed in purple and scarlet, and was glittering with gold, precious stones and pearls. She held a golden cup in her hand, filled with abominable things and the filth of her adulteries. This title was written on her forehead:

MYSTERY
BABYLON THE GREAT
THE MOTHER OF PROSTITUTES
AND OF THE ABOMINATIONS OF THE EARTH

I saw that the woman was drunk with the blood of the saints, the blood of those who bore testimony to Jesus.
REVELATION 17:3–6A (NIV)

Welcome to the city, although this is not exactly a neutral presentation. This is the hyperbolic, hallucinogenic language of apocalypse rather than a holiday brochure. The writer, named as St John, skewers the mega-city of his day, heart of the most powerful empire that his world has known.

Rome, epicentre of civilisation and culture, is portrayed as something like an ultra-sleazy celebrity as well as (in the Hammer Horror final sentence of our Bible reading) a kind of zombie flesh-eater.

Whereas elsewhere in scripture (such as the closing chapters of Ezekiel or the conclusion of Revelation itself) we find descriptions of the redeemed City of God, the new Jerusalem, here we see the Unholy City with all its gaudy veneer of glamour. This Unholy City—Emmanuelle rather than Emmanuel, the city that sets itself up in place of God—recurs throughout the Bible as a pattern of human defiance of heavenly ideals. Think of Babel, Nineveh, Babylon and Corinth—and, tragically, Jerusalem as she turned out under the rule of her succession of corrupt kings, rather than as God intended her to be.

An overly negative portrayal, we might argue. Typical of Christianity, we might say, to caricature the city as a fashionably dressed woman: typically life-denying, culture-denying, sexuality-denying. Not to say sexist—it's too easy simply to condemn a woman for living off immoral earnings! Surely she must have prostituted her daughters only because she lacked a helpful government grant towards pursuing less exploitative ways of earning a living. As Christians should be working to relate faith and contemporary culture, so our focus should be redeeming, rather than shunning, the city and what it represents. And of course we must be careful not to give the impression that Christianity is anti-sex. Gloomy old St John (who wouldn't be a bit grumpy, packed off into exile late in life?) is clearly out to denigrate a stylishly dressed woman who has simply maximised her assets to get a bit of the good life. She picks her outfits with care, enjoys a glass or three of the more esoteric liqueurs, and her sense of style extends to her choice of colour-coordinated transport. (Scarlet outfit, scarlet beast. How 'this season'!)

This is apocalyptic, however—a genre of writing as specific in style as any newspaper diary column. Every word, image and nuance plays a precise part in the carefully constructed whole. Yes, this passage deliberately paints a high-gloss picture of a super-celeb, high society, high fashion demi-goddess. What it all adds up to, though, is the fact that she represents a culture where everything is for sale, everything is ultimately summed up as its cash value, and there are no free gifts. That is the problem, the catch with the special offer that we notice in the small print only after we have signed on the dotted line.

All earthly cities share a few too many of the characteristics of the Unholy City, established as they are on the uncertain foundations of human nature, with its fatal propensity for greed and selfishness. And in the Unholy City, we are of value only to the extent to which we are buying or selling, which depends on our having the means to do so. If we walk its streets penniless or close to penniless, it is a strange experience, because although we can look at everything, we are kept at arm's length. In the Unholy City's marketplace of love, if we lack the ready cash or virtual credit card comprised of charisma, success or whatever is currently considered good looks, we are forced into the role of voyeurs, not permitted to be participants. Even if we are in the enviable position of feeling that our credit is limitless, that we will always have enough put aside to pay the bills (whatever they prove to consist of), our circumstances may change one day. Whether the change comes imperceptibly or with catastrophic speed, we may some day find ourselves over our heads in meta-phorical debt. We face the loss of everything, and all our apologies, tears, pleading and anger will make no difference to the bailiffs at the door.

So, welcome to the city. Welcome to Babylon. Walk with me.

Now, as we walk, darkness has fallen. Office lights are still blazing and computer screens glowing because the global economy doesn't do down-time. Theatre foyers are buzzing; late-night opening at the colossal shopping mall is in full swing; queues snake down the street outside the hottest night clubs. But for us—for everyone with empty wallets and limp handbags—there is no place to go, no connection to make.

Unless.

Come with me, down the dubious-smelling concrete steps, under the subway, across the fitfully lit side-road. There we see him, standing under a streetlight, looking out over the river.

Who is he?

There is something familiar about him. We may suddenly remember him from long ago or we may never have con- sciously met him, yet, beyond reasonable explanation, we know we know him and know that we are known. And when our gaze meets his, it is as if a switch has been pressed. We feel the electric flow of love and acceptance and unbelievable peace. Just for a moment.

He holds out a hand, takes a step towards us, but we feel unready to accept his invitation. Not yet. It is too soon, too scary, too intimate. We want to walk on, and so we do, sensing his eyes still upon us. This we will remember and we may come back to this place, seeking that compelling and loving gaze—and perhaps he will be there.

Then again, perhaps he will not. But something deep inside us whispers that if we seek, we will surely find him one day, quite possibly when and where we least expect.

## For reflection

'Emptiness may be the most important gift we can bring to God, because it leaves space for the free flow of God's grace.'
MARGARET SILF

# 2
## Constant craving

Good morning, Babylon, again.

The working week has finished now; it is Sunday, but it is safe to assume that most of the people we pass on this stroll will not be taking their places for a 10am Eucharist or chivvying the children along to all-age worship at 11. For them, the previous evening's fun has only just ground to a halt and they stumble out into the daylight, past the sardonic bouncers, still surfing the last ripples of a chemical wave, their heads pounding with the all-night beat, groping for taxis in the wincingly bright sunshine and nauseating exhaust fumes on the street.

Others, unseen by us, are surfacing slowly in a tangle of unfamiliar bedclothes, groping through memories of the night before, wondering about the etiquette of dressing and leaving as opposed to dragging out the brief encounter into brunch with strong coffee and newspapers large enough to hide behind.

Embarrassment? Probably. Regret? Quite possibly. But was there love? In the electricity of the midnight embrace, whether on the neon dance floor or the soft-focus studio flat, perhaps there was a deeper connection, body and soul merging into one, even if only momentarily. Maybe… or maybe not. As it happens, our culture offers a selection of ready-made narratives to process such questions, to find a pattern that can lend a bit of meaning and significance to our messy experiences.

There's the story familiar from a host of stylishly depressive films with their keynote shots of decaying high-rises or packed and nervy streets. The soundtrack usually features the latest hit from a singer who sounds appropriately world-weary at 25, their tarnished vocals providing mood-music for a brooding hero or heroine, lip-synching a line about how they regret nothing. Because, in this particular off-the-shelf narrative, the tenuous love connection always breaks, the morning always brings disillusionment and, by Sunday afternoon, the search has resumed for that someone, somewhere, who will provide a lasting fix. Sadly, there is no glimpse of lasting hope, no suggestion that there could be a way through to a new and better place. The closing shot (until the next episode) is of the solitary figure staring out across the cityscape, cigarette glowing in the dusk, coat speckled by the chilly drizzle.

Then there is another kind of narrative that, on the surface at least, offers resolution—a big, bold promise of a proper happy ending. Instead of bleakness and broken connections, it hinges on the romantic clinch, two figures welded together against a sunset backdrop as heavenly musical chords crash around them. They have finally found the One. Oh yes, beyond expectation, they are in the arms of that incredible Other who understands all, forgives all, heals all. Love has taken over and everything and everybody else is forced into second place, no matter what has been sincerely promised at some previous, now regretted and conveniently forgotten time…

Different stories, different takes on similar scenes, but what is inescapable in both is a certain something lurking just out of shot, a disquieting shadow that catches our attention unless we look away quickly. The music fades, the sun sinks into evening cloud, the figures walk away to who knows where—and suddenly the shadow takes solid form and steps out in front of us, threatening to block our way.

It is a monstrous, shadowy presence; it is the terrible hunger of our own hearts.

For despite the allure of the romantic ending or the poignant image of the solitary wanderer pacing through the night, what so often fuels the appetite for such stories, tempting us to place ourselves in this or that role, is the humming energy of that terrible hunger, that monstrous need. Monstrous because it has grown and grown until we can see nothing beyond it, until we are half-crazed by the gnawing desire within. Monstrous because it takes hold of us and squeezes us until we can think of nothing except satisfying that appetite—and, whatever we do, the satisfaction never lasts long enough to give us peace. As the beat of the heart says 'Me, me, me', so the throb of the hunger is 'More, more, more.'

The sun rises and the sun goes down, and hurries to the place where it rises. The wind blows to the south, and goes round to the north; round and round goes the wind, and on its circuits the wind returns. All streams run to the sea, but the sea is not full; to the place where the streams flow, there they continue to flow. All things are wearisome; more than one can express; the eye is not satisfied with seeing, or the ear filled with hearing. What has been is what will be, and what has been done is what will be done; there is nothing new under the sun. Is there a thing of which it is said, 'See, this is new'? It has already been, in the ages before us. The people of long ago are not remembered, nor will there be any remembrance of people yet to come by those who come after them.

ECCLESIASTES 1:5–11

In the words of the 'Teacher', the bleak voice that speaks the book of Ecclesiastes to us down the centuries, there is nothing new under the sun (or the moon, or the streetlights for that matter). Our hollowness and hunger pangs are not unique in the universe. 'See,' the tired voice says to us, 'don't think you're so special.' Look at the world: there is flow and flux built into the system. Why should we be any different, earth-creatures that we are? We sense within us this desperate desire, this hollow craving, and someone or something for a moment offers the illusion of reprieve and completion, but then it all begins again. And again and again and again. In the same way, the cycle of the seasons grinds on, day and night, night and day, summer and winter, winter and summer, on and on and on. There is no end in sight, no release from the cycle, no lasting relief.

In one way, this is comforting. If we look around, we find reminders that others have stood where we stand, and the conclusions they came to are pretty much the conclusions we find ourselves reaching through our own soul-scrutiny. And, as the Teacher tells us, their anguish, however profound it may have been, and even their names, will eventually be forgotten unless everything is inscribed on some particularly hard-wearing surface and in a script that at least one person in the far future will be able to decipher. What we are enduring may seem unrepeatable in its awfulness but, hey, welcome to the human race.

In another way, then, it sounds as if the Teacher is telling us to give up. There is no comfort, no light at the end of the tunnel. The best outcome we can plan and strive for is a decent, muted resignation, graced with a tasteful overlay of philosophical detachment. That, at least, is better than the mess and turmoil of continuing the search. No matter how hard we strive for that decent detachment, however, we will one day relax our guard, hesitate at the wrong moment—and once again the shadow of our desperate neediness will loom over us.

That huge shadow can suck into itself every other face that matters to us, every thought and impulse of our heart, reconfiguring us down to the last nano-particle until we are programmed to play nothing but the obsessive beat of its constant craving. More, more, more.

More what?

That's a rather pointless question to ask in Babylon, because surely we can just focus on the 'more' rather than the 'what'. We should have learned by now that more is good, whatever 'more' it is, so long as it involves active participation in the buoyant, high-risk, high-spend, high-return economy. If the particular 'more' we want happens to be too risky and costly—well, that's our problem, isn't it?

So I suggest we start walking faster, here, now, through the gritty streets of Babylon. I suspect that it's not entirely rational to try to outrun our own shadows, but let's hope that if we keep up a brisk pace and, whatever we do, don't look back, we should be all right.

Just take deep breaths and try not to be afraid, even if you sense darkness rising around you, coming from behind to swallow you whole.

Then we turn a corner and there is the river again, just when we least expect it. Notice, too, that as we have walked and worried, day has turned to night, and now the night has worn away again and the neon-lit clouds have faded to pearly grey with a tiny border of pink. The tidal river is running low and it is tempting to try the ladder leading to the shoreline. It is a little wobbly and more than a little slimy, so take care as you climb down. At the bottom is, surprisingly, sand—a brave little strip of city beach edging the scummy water, conjuring a mental snapshot of long-ago bucket-and-spade holidays.

Washed flat and almost clean by the ebb of the tide, the sand is bare except for a single set of footprints. And—why are we not surprised?—there he is again, ahead of us, waiting. Although it is barely dawn, there is light enough to see his face, recognise his smile. The shadows have gone, for this in-between time, anyway.

When he speaks, we know his voice, although we cannot place his accent. Five words; a question: 'What do you really want?'

It is utterly unanswerable. How can we reply, when hours, days, weeks, months of our lives have been absorbed with wanting, finding, losing, wanting again? Wanting what, really?

We have never asked ourselves that question, have never waited for the answer to bubble up from the very bottom of our consciousness.

Are we ready to do that now?

Not just yet.

## For reflection

'In every story of obsession there is only one character, only one plot. I am writing about myself alone, it's all I know, and for this reason I have always failed in every love, which is to say at the very heart of my life.'

DAMON GALGUT, *IN A STRANGE ROOM*

# 3
# Broken

Sorry about this: our walk has brought us to a place where no visitors ever come, unless they are refuse collectors, social workers or the emergency services. If the architecture looks familiar but you can't quite place a context, think Stalin's Soviet Union or Ceausescu's Romania. Designed and built, we presume, as a concrete and glass utopia for a happy and hardworking proletariat, these buildings are now unlikely survivors in a very different future, battered, mostly boarded-up, and waiting for the wrecking ball.

Sorry again: the lifts are not working, although I'm not sure you would want to use one anyway. The stairs are not much better but at least we are not confined up-close with the graffiti, the used needles and the smell. Come with me, up the stained steps, past the litter blown into the corners, cautiously peering to right and left before venturing out along the walkways. Believe it or not, there is somebody for us to meet here, although we may have to knock for a while on the steel security door before it opens to us. Some days it will not open at all, so let's hope that today is a good day.

Here's relief of a kind: the door has opened and we have been permitted to step inside. The flat is dim because the light bulb is weak and the curtains are pulled shut, on a shoddy track tied up with string. It seems that no daylight is allowed in here, not even on a heavily clouded afternoon like this. No matter: we can see that the few rooms are more than tidy. They are almost bare, with virtually no sign of present occupation, although somebody must have opened the door.

There is the 'somebody'—that figure now curled up again in the chair in the corner of the lounge, hands folding and unfolding nervously in their lap.

It is hard to tell this person's age; hard to find out who they are and why they are sitting here alone with the curtains closed on a workday afternoon. We cannot even ask just now because their face is turned away and they are crying. Not sobbing noisily or just a little choked up for a minute, but with tears that are falling steadily and almost noiselessly, as if they have done so (and I fear that they have) for hours.

After a while, in among the tears, we begin to hear words, a thread of sound that catches every now and then in the throat. The words tell a story that hurts the heart to hear, one of vulnerability trampled on, trust betrayed; apparently nobody else had noticed or, if they had noticed, cared enough to intervene. It is all desperately miserable, a complete and total mess; we want to interrupt, commiserate, do something brisk and efficient to sort it out. Open the curtains, for a start.

But as we move, the figure in the chair looks up for the first time. What we see then stops us dead. It is impossible—nightmarishly so—but somehow or other, the face looking back at us is one we recognise.

It may be the face of one we have shamefully forgotten, but, as we stare at them and they stare back, we find that we start to recall them with uncomfortable clarity, along with incidents we regret, words we should not have said, decisions we should have made differently. Maybe, of course, the part we played in their life was no more than a small wounding, almost overlooked in the larger landscape of their pain, but, small or not, intentional or not, wounding there was. For this person we were a means of hurt, not of grace and blessing.

It may be a face that we know far, far too well and have tried hard to put from our minds, filing under 'Mistakes: not to be revisited'. We know that we did great and deliberate harm to them, while never intending, of course, that the later circumstances of life might bring them to this place, this situation.

Then again, there could be something about the face that, most disconcertingly of all, reminds us of our own. Is this what we are really like, inside, when the doors and curtains are closed and our public mask is removed? Perhaps those tears are really ours, stored within if not actually shed. Perhaps this dereliction is where we feel we belong, because it is no worse than we deserve.

[Job said] 'Why is light given to those in misery, and life to the bitter of soul, to those who long for death that does not come, who search for it more than for hidden treasure, who are filled with gladness and rejoice when they reach the grave? Why is light given to a man whose way is hidden, whom God has hedged in? For sighing comes to me instead of food; my groans pour out like water. What I feared has come upon me; what I dreaded has happened to me. I have no peace, no quietness; I have no rest, but only turmoil... What strength do I have, that I should still hope? What prospects, that I should be patient? Do I have the strength of stone? Is my flesh bronze? Do I have any power to help myself, now that success has been driven from me?'
JOB 3:20–26; 6:11–13 (NIV)

For generations more Bible-literate than today's, 'Job's com-forters' meant those whose response to suffering was to tell the sufferer to sit up and stop feeling sorry for themselves. The book of Job is one of the most troubling in scripture, because it tells of a good and God-fearing man who nevertheless loses everything, and through no fault of his own. His family is murdered, his wealth obliterated, his health destroyed, and all his friends can say is, in effect, 'You must have done something wrong, because God does not allow bad things to happen to good people.' While there is a happy ending after chapter after chapter of anguish, no clear answer is given to Job's question: 'Why me?'

For those who prefer life and faith tidy, with every loose end sewn up or at least knotted neatly, Job's story is problematic, best moved over swiftly, along with those many other troubling bits of the Bible. Or perhaps the answer is to mentally patch in the nice 'I know that my Redeemer lives' verses: they, at least, are something that every good Christian can affirm with due confidence, not to mention bringing to mind Handel's lovely aria.

For those whose life and faith have split apart, though, who are blinking in the aftermath or in mid-maelstrom of catastrophe, the tortured words of Job show that the depths of despair can be voiced in the presence of God, although the speaker may have lost hope that anybody will bother to listen, let alone help. The very act of putting their thoughts and feelings into words can be a tiny twitch of positive energy, an honest acknowledgment of how things truly are, even if those words are never spoken aloud.

Whether anybody can bear to hear those words is another matter. Job's friends certainly could not bear to hear him without reproach. The sight of a distress flare far out on a stormy sea can terrify the casual onlooker, implying responsibility for rescue. Fair enough if that onlooker happens to be an experienced coastguard, but a non-expert witness may well panic. What should they do? Chances are, they'll take the wrong decision and whatever disaster follows will be their fault. Not enough people seem to realise that the smallest gesture of kindness and concern can be a lifesaver in so many senses of the word. To the one lost in the storm, it can be the answering signal from the shore: 'You are not alone. Your distress has been noticed. Help is coming. Hold on.'

It is only the one who has abandoned any hope of rescue who stops looking for help. The one who still wants to live will not give up, even though their voice may be too hoarse to call out any longer. While their strength holds, they will be swimming as strongly as they can, eyes scanning the horizon, just in case.

Sadly, though, the worse the situation, the greater the risk of a fearful response from the onlooker, especially if that onlooker fundamentally doubts their ability to help or rescue anybody—even more especially if the suffering they witness is, at least in part, the consequence of something they have done. When that is the case, acknowledging the extent of help required involves acknowledging the extent of the wrong done—and that is a step they may yet be unable to take.

Here, now, in this miserable and airless room, we do not know what action to take. We seem to have nothing to offer except half-baked good wishes and platitudes. All we can do is linger uselessly in the doorway, unsure whether it is right to go, quite certain that there is no way we can help. Probably better to slip away quietly, under the circumstances…

'I tell you—everything will be all right.'

How did he get in here? Who forgot to shut the door?

No one saw him enter, but here he is, brushing past us, paying no attention to anybody except the figure in the chair.

He walks over, kneels down and reaches out to fold his arms around them.

'Don't be afraid.'

They are looking at one another now, and his grin is lighting up the room. With superb dramatic timing, the shoddy curtain track falls from the window so that golden light pours in. The clearing sky is radiant.

Then, hand in hand, without another word, the two of them leave together, footsteps echoing along the walkway to the stairs, fading into the non-silence of Babylon. They have gone—but before we can think about following, shouts are heard from another direction, disturbingly close at hand. Sirens are sounding, and down below, among the broken glass and crushed lager cans, a couple of police cars screech to a standstill. Trouble is kicking off in the neighbourhood, as it does most days about this time.

Time for us to go, too, I think.

## For reflection

'Divine love is incessantly restless until it turns all woundedness into health, all deformity into beauty, all embarrassment into laughter. In biblical faith, brokenness is never celebrated as an end in itself. God's brokenness is but an expression of a love on its way to completion.'

BELDEN LANE, *THE SOLACE OF FIERCE LANDSCAPES*

# 4
# The hidden garden

Sometimes we begin to fear that the streets of Babylon are endless. Perhaps we will walk and walk and walk and never come to the edge, beyond the trailing mess of ring roads, industrial estates and retail parks. Sometimes, however acclimatised we are to the incessant noise and rush of the city, we sense the beginnings of panic, a sudden and desperate urge to breathe air that smells of wet leaves, to hear birdsong, see the stars. Sometimes the tension builds to a high-pitched scream in our heads, so that before long we are walking with fists clenched in our coat pockets, shoulders straining with tension. We are on a jostling train platform or fighting to board a bus or buffeted by impatient crowds in the marketplace, and suddenly adrenalin winds us to snapping point, until we find a deranged audio loop running through our heads: 'If you—look at me like that, I'll—punch your—face. If you—dare to—touch me, I'll—destroy you.'

Babylon has infected us, burrowed its way right inside and lodged, parasitic, in our guts. This is very bad news.

Time to stop and find a space to rest, and let the rage burn itself out until we are limp and calm. We may not be sure what can or should happen after that, but limp and calm sounds like a reasonable starting-point. Better than glassy-eyed, foam-flecked madness, anyway.

I know a place; walk with me. It sounds unlikely, I admit, but if we turn down this side-road, past the 1950s maison-ettes, the old fire station turned designer flats, the derelict pool hall and the gastropub, we will eventually see some elaborate iron gates set in a crumbling stone wall. Push them—they will open—and we can pass through.

Here we are: a garden, hidden in the heart of the city. The rose beds are a little overgrown but still blossoming and perfumed; notice the stone pedestal that once held a sundial but now operates as a bird table. The grass is speckled with daisies and buttercups, and in the corner is a tidy compost heap, that key feature of community eco-projects. But look beyond these and you will be surprised again. At the far end of the garden is a short flight of steps behind security fencing, and at the top of the steps is a life-size wooden crucifix. Where the garden now grows, a church once stood, burned to the ground years ago.

There are few left alive now who remember it as it was, but others came along over time and saw the ruins and cared enough to reclaim a patch of bare ground from the spoil-heaps of sooty brick and charred wood. Then they planted a garden.

At first glance, the crucifix appears quite forgotten, cut off behind the wire and attended only by bright splashes of fireweed and nettles grown so tall that they are toppling over. If we go closer, though, we will see that someone has clumsily splashed red paint on the head, hands and feet of the hanging figure, to give a touch of gory realism to the weather-worn wood. Go closer still, and we see that petitioners and penitents, and those wanting to make some gesture of thanks to somebody, have come here to tie their tokens to the fence. Faded ribbons and little medals stir in the breeze; drooping flowers are fastened next to palm crosses, and a selection of cuddly toys smile through masks of grime.

We cannot climb the steps to touch the nailed feet, but we can stand at the fence and look at the wooden face. Beneath the paint splashes, despite the blurring effect of 70-odd years of wind, rain and sun, the grief and pain expressed in the contorted features is still clear enough to touch those who pause long enough to notice. We can see that this is one who knew what it meant to be broken-hearted.

> They heard the sound of the Lord God walking in the garden at the time of the evening breeze, and the man and his wife hid themselves from the presence of the Lord God among the trees of the garden. But the Lord God called to the man, and said to him, 'Where are you?' He said, 'I heard the sound of you in the garden, and I was afraid, because I was naked; and I hid myself.' He said, 'Who told you that you were naked? Have you eaten from the tree of which I commanded you not to eat?' The man said, 'The woman whom you gave to be with me, she gave me fruit from the tree, and I ate.' Then the Lord God said to the woman, 'What is this that you have done?' The woman said, 'The serpent tricked me, and I ate.'
>
> GENESIS 3:8–13

In the opening act of the Bible story, God creates the world. As the finishing touch, the icing on the delectable cake, the story tells us that he made human beings, man and woman. And, so the story goes on, God made a garden. This garden was not planted in an effort to patch up ruins but as a literal flowering of creativity and harnessed beauty, planted near the junction of four great rivers, two of which are still marked on maps today: Pishon and Gihon, Tigris and Euphrates.

In a hot and dry climate, one of the ultimate luxuries is a lush, secluded garden, hidden away behind high walls and tantalising the dusty alleyways beyond with a glimpse of greenery and the whisper of a fountain. Visit any garden centre today, even in a mild and rainy part of the world, and you will see reminders of this dream, the promise of a garden paradise, albeit at the cost of a lot of heavy labour (which always seems to end up longer and heavier than the TV makeover shows promise). Imagine, then, the privilege of a garden designed and planted by the Almighty himself. This, as the story tells it, was the birthday gift prepared for the man and his wife, firstborn of creation, a place where they could live in peace and delight and gradually grow in wisdom as they strolled each day with their Creator in the evening cool. They were subject to just one ground-rule, to do with one special tree.

Just a single rule: do not eat the fruit of that special tree. There were plenty of other fruits to choose from, so surely this limited restriction was no great hardship.

So you would think.

But what we have here is the awful unravelling of relationship. Whether or not you uphold a literal reading of the Eden story, whether or not you believe that there was an actual garden with two human residents, a snake and God strolling out to meet them, the emotions expressed in our Bible passage are as raw and fresh as any soap opera, despite (or maybe because of) the terse phrasing and limited descriptive detail. Temptation to break the rules was followed by transgression, which was followed by shame, blame, guilt and the desire—no, the necessity—for concealment. But how can anyone conceal themselves from the eternal God?

We know this story. Even if we can't quote the Genesis account verbatim, we know the story because the same narrative is repeated over and over again in history, in society today, in the lives of our friends, our families and ourselves.

We know what we should not do; we do it anyway; we suffer the consequences.

It is as if we are entrusted with a beautiful and fragile gift—priceless, yet entrusted to us to cherish. All we have to do is hold it carefully and find a safe place to keep it. Instead, though, it is all too easy to take it for granted, to grasp it carelessly; and, before we realise what is happening, it falls from our hands and shatters on the ground. Then we are on our knees, broken-hearted, trying to gather up the pieces, sifting debris from the dust, trying to deny the stark fact that it is broken, irretrievable.

Everything is lost…

Not quite.

Even though the man and the woman had to leave the garden, never to return, the story goes on to tell how God made the first clothes to cover their shame and nakedness. Even though his children had rejected him and the relationship he had established with them (a grievous pattern of covenant-making followed by covenant-breaking that repeats throughout scripture), he did not abandon them. They reaped the consequences of their wrongful choices—yet, despite no mention of conscious repentance on their part, God was at work to mend the damage, weaving a golden thread of grace that works through and knits together the jagged lines of making and breaking. Not because the man and the woman deserved it, but because he loved them.

As we loiter in our sanctuary garden, staring at the blurred wooden face of the one on the cross, we may sense within us a profound longing for such mending, such grace. We feel that we have lost everything that once mattered to us through our own deliberate fault, or through the deliberate act of another. On the other hand, we may not be conscious of any great loss or emptiness but know that we long to feel held by a love as tender and steadfast as the love of God for the man and the woman. We may be broken-hearted; we may simply feel a little lonely and lost. Either way, something compels us to step forward and touch the wire fence that guards the crucifix, perhaps add our own token to those hanging there, perhaps try to recall some form of prayer. May as well try anything once...

In that moment, without looking round, we know who has come to stand at our shoulder. Clearly his presence is inescapable, no matter how far and how long we walk in the city. There is a pause, time enough for a long sigh, and once again he speaks.

'Come with me.'

This time we follow, because we have finally come to the point of admitting that there is nothing else left for us to do.

## For reflection

'It is because we believe in God's unconditional love and forgiveness that we may dare to open our eyes to the hurt and the harm of our actions and not panic... Sorrow is a healthy awareness of the harm we have caused others and ourselves, whereas feelings of guilt can be a narcissistic concentration on myself.'

TIMOTHY RADCLIFFE, WHY GO TO CHURCH?

# 5
## Found

Where do we go when we finally decide to follow this singular individual who turns up again and again as we wander the ways and byways of the city? What we will discover is that the place where he leads us is always the safest possible place, even if the route there takes us along dark and difficult roads. No matter how troubling the journey, he is always walking just ahead of us; we do not have to worry about losing our way, getting left behind and lost. Even when we have to pause, footsore and tired as we now are, he pauses too and waits patiently for us to be ready to continue.

Now, at last, we have reached the door of that safest place. Before we even pass through, an instinct tells us that this could well be home, somewhere we have been seeking for longer than we can remember, or a place we once had, but lost, for whatever reason. A place neither too grand nor too stylish, neither too cramped nor too shabby, but warm and welcoming, with room enough for everyone who wants to come in.

Over the threshold (no turning back now) and here is a safe space where we can put down everything we have been carrying, all that is weighing us down, even if it is very important to us, and even if we have been carrying it for a very, very long time. Cloakroom on the left; down the corridor and here is the kitchen, where we can sit at ease, even sprawl, in front of the fire. We can take the food and drink held out to us, although our automatic response may be, 'Oh, no thank you, I'm all right.' Take and eat. Drink. It is ours to enjoy.

But this is the moment that we have feared and dreaded, when surely we must begin our defence of ourselves, our justification of the wrongs we have done and the good we have not done, the painful probing of our desires.

Choosing to admit that we need forgiveness is probably one of the hardest decisions we ever have to face. In our society, the talk tends to revolve around defending rights and identifying victims. There is always somebody else to blame for our actions—our family background, our social and economic circumstances, even our church, our God. Events come together in such a way as to bestow what appears to be unassailable 'victim' status upon us, but we should be cautious about accepting such a designation, lest it stop us thoroughly examining our own actions and attitudes, either now or in the future. It is one thing to be clear-eyed about harm done to us and the subsequent repair work required; it is quite another to adopt the attitude that henceforth we are for ever to be treated with kid gloves and never called to account in any way whatsoever.

It is very tempting to construct defences against acknowledging fault, because it involves enormous vulnerability. Taking off our carefully pieced-together body armour, emerging from our painstakingly grown shell, means that we are naked and ashamed. We have no defence against ridicule and rejection. Why subject ourselves to such scrutiny, put ourselves at risk of such trauma, if we can more or less get by as we are, thank you? Surely it is better to skimp on the honesty and present our most attractive and acceptable aspect, to other people, to God or even to ourselves.

We have to be conscious of the fact that 'getting by' is less than God would wish for his beloved children, however. Perhaps it is the best that we have been able to manage for quite a while (months? years? decades?) but we have to remain open to the fact that an unprecedented opportunity for renewal and change may suddenly present itself.

Then what are we to do?

Now the tax collectors and 'sinners' were all gathering round to hear [Jesus]. But the Pharisees and the teachers of the law muttered, 'This man welcomes sinners and eats with them.' Then Jesus told them this parable: 'Suppose one of you has a hundred sheep and loses one of them. Does he not leave the ninety-nine in the open country and go after the lost sheep until he finds it? And when he finds it, he joyfully puts it on his shoulders and goes home. Then he calls his friends and neighbours together and says, "Rejoice with me; I have found my lost sheep." I tell you that in the same way there will be more rejoicing in heaven over one sinner who repents than over ninety-nine righteous persons who do not need to repent.'
LUKE 15:1–7 (NIV)

Of Jesus' 'lost and found' stories, people generally seem to know and quote most often the one about the runaway (aka 'prodigal' or spendthrift) son. It has such a compelling and contemporary plot-line with richly drawn characters—the headstrong young man who defies convention and goes off to enjoy himself abroad somewhere, leaving his law-abiding brother behind. When his new life goes wrong and he is left with nothing, he comes to his senses and decides to return home. Cue dramatic reconciliation scene, with the loving father defying social convention to run out and meet the returning penitent, not with curses but with embraces and the promise of a party to end all parties. Then cue entry of disgruntled brother...

The story of the lost sheep is, in some ways, rather less frequently cited. Maybe the fact that the focus is on an animal (a woolly and endearing animal, at that) means that it is prone to be limited to the category of Sunday school lesson material or nice subject for a Bible story picturebook. There is less chance of tricky questions from inquisitive children ('What exactly did the prodigal son spend his money on? What sort of friends?') but plenty of possibilities for an attractively illustrated gift or an easy quiz answer as to the identity of the shepherd.

We should not forget, either, that Jesus' other story in the same chapter of Luke's Gospel tells of a woman hunting for a missing coin. While the runaway son makes the deliberate choice to leave home and also to return, neither the coin nor the sheep chooses to be lost. They do what comes naturally to them—and getting lost is the consequence. The coin, being small and hard, bounces and rolls into a dark corner after falling to the ground; the sheep wanders away and becomes separated from the rest of the flock, not through wilfulness or the deliberate seeking of adventure, but presumably because the grass looked greener in the distance and it felt hungry.

Those who are respectable and law-abiding are openly troubled by Jesus' tendency to act as if respectability and rule-keeping do not matter. The three stories that he tells in response to their muttering all show, in a variety of ways, God's attitude towards one who is lost, separated from the flock and far from home. God is a hard-working shepherd who does not spare himself in caring for his animals. He is also a woman ransacking her house for a lost treasure, and a forgiving father. The Pharisees and teachers of the law here (or, to reach for a modern-day equivalent, some church leaders and campaigners for Christian moral standards in society) clearly struggle to grasp an iota of the love of God. While he is, of course, pleased that so many serve him faithfully and strive to live by his commandments, we cannot overlook the outrageous punchline of the sheep story: 'There will be more rejoicing in heaven over one sinner who repents than over ninety-nine righteous persons who do not need to repent.'

Two facts must be held in continual tension by every one of us who has decided to follow the way of Christ: we are all forgiven sinners; we are all God's beloved children. At the same time, those who live in the knowledge that they have been forgiven much may well be blessed with a deeper awareness of the grace and love of God. This is surely because they have seen the powerfully transformative effects of this grace and love in their own lives.

Before we can come to the point of freely admitting our sinfulness and selfishness, we have to be in a place where we feel secure. We have to be able to relax in the assurance that we have been found, that we are not on our own, and that we are now being strengthened with the strength of God to continue the necessary journey of healing and forgiveness.

Sitting—lounging—in the warm heart of this place that we recognise as home, we can be at rest. The room is so still that we can distinguish every separate, small sound that makes up the whole, peaceful silence. The fire in the stove crackles from time to time; the sofa where we sprawl is comfortable; the blanket that has been draped around our shoulders is soft. Perhaps, if we do not move and if we hold our breath, we can suspend this moment in time and then we will be safe always.

We cannot forget the one sitting opposite us, though,

in the old rocking-chair that creaks as he shifts position a little and smiles at us. This must be the moment that we have dreaded, when we have to go through some harrowing emotional scene with tears and hand-wringing. It would be far easier not to do that. Do we really have the energy? It would be far easier to get to our feet, let the blanket slip to the floor, offer our thanks and go. Perhaps there'll be another, more convenient time for whatever seems about to happen, to happen.

But it would appear that there is no pre-existing script to follow—not here, not now.

'Please don't leave yet.' His eyes are so kind. 'Let's spend some time together, just chatting about this and that.'

The love and acceptance are devastating in their effectiveness, far more so than any amount of frowning or shouting. It seems we really have no choice but to stay. Hesitantly, we begin to talk, just about this and that for now, but it is a start.

## For reflection

'Sometimes God's blessing comes not as a complete solution to our needs or an infusion of unspeakable joy, but as the beginning of new life, the sense that we have turned the corner and that movement is possible where previously we were boxed in, that hope is budding.'
CHRISTOPHER COCKSWORTH AND ROSALIND BROWN, *BEING A PRIEST TODAY*

Part Two

# Because he first loved us

# 6
# He chose her

We have wandered the city together; we have come to a place which is the very definition of 'safe house'. We have eaten and drunk in the presence of the one who has brought us here; we have rested; we have begun to talk. Now we are ready to stretch our legs a little, being free to wander the corridors, up and down flights of stairs, going pretty much where we please.

So many doors... which one shall we try first?

The china doorknob is cool to the touch; the hinges creak a little. The door opens and we find ourselves in a library. Shelf after shelf of books reach up to a gallery and, beyond that, to the ceiling, stretching from wall to wall. We see not only traditional leather-bound spines but also colourful paperbacks jammed in beside them. In every alcove there is a comfortable armchair, some with a stack of volumes beside them, as if the readers are about to return at any moment.

This is a place for us to sit and rest, because it is time for us to hear a story—a love story, as it happens, but one from long ago and far away, from a quite different world and time. If we hear it somewhat adapted, we may connect better with its unfamiliar contours and startling progression of emotions. Then it may begin to help us glimpse something of a love so startlingly huge and enduring that it is, to tell the truth, beyond human comprehension.

Listen with me...

A young man—late teens? early 20s?—is walking his dog across a playing field on the edge of a small town. It is an early midsummer morning; the sun is warm and the air full of birdsong. Life feels good and the prospect of the working day invigorating for this particular young man. He throws a tennis ball for his dog, who leaps after it joyfully, catches it in mid-air and rushes it back to his master, then waits, quivering with excitement, for it to sail through the air again.

Off it goes, a bit too far this time, so that it lands in the lush undergrowth beneath the trees by the river, which borders one side of the field. The dog streaks after it and disappears from view. The young man ambles in the same direction—and stops. Above the birdsong he hears something else, a disturbing noise that he cannot place. It sounds a bit like a newborn lamb, but it can't be, not in June, not in the woods by the river. The dog emerges again, excited, urgent, tail communicating a thrilling discovery, and the young man follows it through the nettles and wild flowers to a smooth hollow of bare ground beneath an oak tree. And there he sees what he least expects—arms and legs flailing feebly, naked skin damp with dew, crying the high-pitched, apparently inconsolable cry of the very newborn.

A baby girl, abandoned.

This young man, for all his youth, knows what to do. He pulls off his T-shirt, gently scoops the baby up, not forgetting to support her head, and wraps her securely. Holding her close to his chest, so that his warmth and heartbeat start to soothe her, he calls the dog to heel and sets off to find help.

Help is found and care arranged for the baby, but, despite everybody's best efforts, the mother is never traced. The girl is a foundling, abandoned hours after birth, an unwanted arrival. Something about her touches the young man to the heart; he finds that he cannot forget her. Every year, on the anniversary of her discovery, he sends a card and gifts. Sometimes he visits the family who took her in and brought her up as their own.

Years pass.

Then an anniversary day comes, more than 20 years later. The young man has matured almost to mid-life; he has worked hard, prospered, but somehow never found a life partner. Invited for a celebration lunch at the family home, he arrives a little early and glimpses his one-time foundling out in the garden, picking flowers for the table. He has known her for so long but, suddenly, on this anniversary day, he sees her as if for the first time, as she is now. And when she turns and smiles at him, he is astonished to realise that he is attracted to her, as one adult to another.

On the day you were born your navel cord was not cut, nor were you washed with water to cleanse you, nor rubbed with salt, nor wrapped in cloths. No eye pitied you, to do any of these things for you out of compassion for you; but you were thrown out in the open field, for you were abhorred on the day you were born. I passed by you, and saw you flailing about in your blood. As you lay in your blood, I said to you, 'Live! and grow up like a plant of the field.' You grew up and became tall and arrived at full womanhood; your breasts were formed, and your hair had grown; yet you were naked and bare. I passed by you again and looked on you; you were at the age for love.'
Ezekiel 16:4–8a

This is a strange and startling story to find in scripture, but here it is, in Ezekiel, one of the more mystifying and less familiar of the Old Testament prophets as far as most people are concerned. Ezekiel was carried off to a valley of dry bones, had to eat a scroll and was obliged to lie on his side for an impossibly tedious amount of time just to make a statement to God's disobedient people. Gift of prophecy, anyone?

The story that this prophet tells in chapter 16 is a long, at times painfully extended metaphor about the troubled relationship between God and his chosen nation. The people are represented by 'Jerusalem', the earthly city that is depicted as a woman, destined to be the consort of the narrator. Commentaries can help to explain some of the more obscure details, which relate to the history of Jerusalem and the kingdom of Judah, of which Jerusalem became the capital after the kingdom of Israel divided. Even if we struggle to make sense of some of the imagery, however, the emotional force of the narrative is compelling.

When we think of an abandoned newborn baby, we probably assume it is a matter of course that we should want to rescue and protect it. Yet, less than 300 years ago, Thomas Coram, a retired sea captain, was inspired to set up a home for foundlings because he was so appalled by the number of abandoned babies he saw literally on the streets of London. In parts of the ancient Near East, as in other societies at various times, the exposure of unwanted infants (especially girls) would have been a known practice. We should not imagine that the concern shown for the baby would have been deemed the expected behaviour at that time. The prophet weaves it into his story to make a dramatic point about the strength of God's love and care for Jerusalem.

The child grows to maturity—and it is at this point that our modern sensibilities are disturbed. An older man looking with adult longing at a young woman, naked, in a field? Remember: this is metaphor stretched to fit a particular set of historical circumstances. There is no implication of abuse or inappropriate intimacy: the baby girl is now adult but she is still uncared-for, unclaimed, without a family to protect her from harm. The point in hand is that there was nothing particular about Jerusalem to mark the city out as special; beauty was truly in the eyes of the beholder. As the storytelling prophet describes it, God passes by again and sees that she is 'at the age for love', in the coy phrase of the English translators. (The original Hebrew focuses explicitly on her newly acquired womanly attributes.)

We should remember, by the way, that the idea of intense romantic feelings as the essential precursor to marriage is a relatively recent development in the history of humankind. In the culture of the time, as in many cultures around the world today, marriage was a contract, a carefully planned arrangement by two families to cement certain social or even business relationships. The feelings would (or, sadly, in some cases would not) have followed on from the commitment, rather than the other way round.

What makes love, desire, grow—or, as sometimes happens, burst into full and vigorous life at little more than the meeting of a glance? In some cases, we can trace cause and effect, discover connections that were grasped by the body and soul long before the head understood what was going on. Here the male speaker looks at the young woman and notes, candidly, that she is physically ready for love. She is also in evident need of care and protection, and we will see as the story unfolds how he chooses to take on that caring and protecting role, instead of simply using the young woman for a moment or two of pleasure and then leaving her in the field as he found her. He takes her as his wife, not because she is the most important or wealthy or well-dressed young woman available but because he wants to do so. Why? The mystery is not explained; love cannot always be explained.

Over the years, too many people have tied themselves in too many knots, trying to clarify, in a 'chicken and egg' sort of way, whether we choose to follow God through an act of purely autonomous will or whether our decision can only be made because we have been chosen by him first. We may worry that if he has chosen us, the choice implies that he has refused to choose others—yet surely he can't choose everyone? Although this is another mystery that is never fully explained in scripture, the prophet's story states clearly that in this case, the initiative was God's: he saw, and he chose to embark on a relationship. The challenge of the story (as we shall see) lies in the response of the one chosen and loved.

Of course, this is picture language—the prophet's story, like our present-day story of the man finding the baby by the edge of the playing-field. Our words, however carefully selected and nuanced, can only hint at the outermost borders of all that God has been, is and always will be. In many ways, it is easier to speak of what God is not, rather than trying to speak of what he is. But although we must not say 'God is a man' or even 'God is human', we can say truthfully that 'there is something of God in us', the image (we might say, fingerprint) of the Creator. And scripture shows us that the bond between Creator and creature is fundamentally—on the Creator's side, at least—a bond of love.

## For reflection

'The love of God... while inherent in creation and in human beings, comes as a gift of grace to those who are prepared to embark on the way of divine love.'

ANDREW CLITHEROW, *DESIRE, LOVE AND THE RULE OF ST BENEDICT*

# 7
## He cherished her

However unsettling certain aspects of our story may be, our surroundings soothe us as we listen (if we like libraries in the old style, that is). Through the half-open door, from down the corridor, we can hear a grandfather clock ticking; somewhere a window is open, bringing a thin current of air and a waft of floor polish and dusty books. So many books—although it can be argued that there is only a limited number of different plots, and that recurring patterns of characters and events are reshaped and adapted as the occasion demands.

The pattern of love stories is familiar enough as we look back over the centuries and across cultures. If there is choice, linked closely to commitment, and a mixture of tenderness, desire and affection in a context of mutual attraction, surely it is not too much to hope for a reassuringly happy ending?

Whatever the exact plot-line, whether we are talking fact or fantasy, love almost always comes as a gift, a 'falling in love' moment of epiphany, even when an individual has put in a lot of work beforehand to cultivate it. And even if we intentionally invest emotional capital in a relationship, hoping that it will offer space and opportunity for love to grow, the wonder of reciprocity, the mystery of two people becoming mutually captivated by one another—especially when the possibility of such connection seems, to all appearances, highly unlikely—well, that is an astonishing gift.

Listen with me, then, as our unusual love story continues…

They have known each other for so long, yet there is a bit of awkwardness between the man and the young woman on that anniversary day. When they talk about it much later, it turns out that they both knew something had changed in their relationship, suddenly and unexpectedly, and for a while both hesitated over the next move. So, on that day, when the time comes to say goodbye, he stands on the doorstep and hugs her for a moment longer than he ever has before, and a breeze blows strands of her long hair across his face. As they step away from each other, her eyes hold his gaze a moment longer than they ever have before, and then they both begin to smile. Both guess what has started to happen.

In the following days, weeks, months, he feels as if the smiling never stops. After so long, and a fair few false starts, he has finally made a choice and is preparing to make a commitment to another. Everybody expresses their happiness—well, nearly everybody. Some are a little guarded in their response but he reckons that is only to be expected, given the way events have turned out. It feels like a story from the happier writings of Shakespeare or Dickens—the guardian finally recognising his love for his ward. Tenderness, desire and affection, a trinity of loving feelings, bless his every move and transfigure everything he sees.

At last he has somebody to shower with gifts, using the money that has piled up unspent over the years. She is an appreciative recipient of earrings, necklaces, perfume, stylish clothes and expensive shoes, as she responds to his love with—at first—astonishment and gratitude. Then he starts to note, with some amusement, how well she knows her own mind. Although she is still young, she is very determined and has developed a clear sense of how things ought to be. He is happy to indulge her choices and ideas because he loves the way she rises to every new occasion, every new challenge, with enormous energy, her self-confidence growing hour by hour.

One day she actually writes him a love letter instead of the usual texts and emails, to be (so she tells him) like long-ago lovers, and he carries it around with him in his pocket so that he can read certain phrases, even if they are a little hackneyed, again and again: 'I will do everything I can to make you happy and proud of me... You are the nicest, most amazing person I have ever met... I never thought anything as wonderful as you could happen to me... What we have will last for ever.' Every time he thinks of her, longing shakes him to the core; he cannot wait to be with her again.

The night before the wedding, he stands at his bedroom window and gazes in the direction of the place where she lives, willing time to pass. His mobile phone buzzes—a final text from her: 'Till this time tomorrow! XXXX' A mixture of relief, joy and excitement surges in and around him and he shakes his head at the tears rolling down his cheeks.

I spread the edge of my cloak over you, and covered your nakedness: I pledged myself to you and entered into a covenant with you, says the Lord God, and you became mine. Then I bathed you with water and washed off the blood from you, and anointed you with oil. I clothed you with embroidered cloth and with sandals of fine leather; I bound you in fine linen and covered you with rich fabric. I adorned you with ornaments... You were adorned with gold and silver, while your clothing was of fine linen, rich fabric, and embroidered cloth. You had choice flour and honey and oil for food.

> You grew exceedingly beautiful, fit to be a queen. Your fame
> spread among the nations on account of your beauty.
> EZEKIEL 16:8B–14A (ABRIDGED)

Remember the story of Ruth and Boaz, the widowed foreigner
who wins the love of the wealthy landowner? In that story,
as in Ezekiel's tale here, the spreading of the man's cloak
over the woman was the quintessential sign of kinship and
protection, in a society where having such protection was
pretty much the only way that women could hope to live
in security and peace. As in the story of Ruth and Boaz, the
act of covering takes place in a field. Unlike Ruth, however,
'Jerusalem' has been utterly vulnerable—naked, bloodied,
without a single protective kinship relationship to safeguard
her.

Until now.

Now she is given the finest of everything—clothing, cos-
metics, jewellery, food and drink. Her newly acquired husband
has chosen not just to meet her physical needs in an everyday
kind of way, keeping her clothed, fed and shod, but to treat
her like a queen. In accordance with the covenant that he has
made with her, he cares for her in a manner that would surely
surpass any expectations. The lost girl is treated like royalty,
even though there is nothing about her situation or parentage,
as earlier verses in the Bible passage make clear, to warrant such
status. As a result, she becomes a great and famous beauty.

This story is a staggering contrast to some of the stories
told in the ancient Near East about other gods, so many of
whom spent so much time seducing (or just raping) beautiful
mortal women, because that was how the mood took them.
No time for niceties such as covenant and commitment, but
a quick change of shape (swan, shower of gold, the husband

of the woman in question...) and Zeus, for one, had his way. By contrast, the action of the God of scripture is the making of covenant, the act of marriage—but he does not just love his consort, Jerusalem, for her mind or her personality. He delights in her physical beauty, in adorning her body, proud of what his beloved wife has become through his cherishing.

The context for such cherishing is, of course, mutually binding commitment. They belong to one another and to no other. Thus the way is opened for the deepest sharing, the most profound vulnerability, the 'knowing' that is the term used in some Bible translations for the sexual expression of love. Is it disturbing to think of God loving his people with a love that encompasses all that and more? We are accustomed to thinking of 'our heavenly Father' and 'Jesus our Brother' but we should not forget that, from time to time in scripture, we come across passages that speak of God delighting in his people in a way that is by no means exclusively parental. We may be familiar with the idea of the Church as the 'bride of Christ' but do we stop and wonder what the wedding night might involve? Does it occur to us that there might be a wedding night at all? Perhaps such a train of thought sounds too shockingly erotic, and so, we assume, it can have nothing whatever to do with our understanding of the Christian faith.

Certainly many mystics (Teresa of Avila, for example) employed the language of ecstasy in a way that wove together physical, spiritual and emotional experiences to express their feelings about God. We may find such language a bit embarrassing or be tempted to dismiss it as a sign of an over-active imagination, but we shouldn't limit the ways we talk about our Creator to purely rational discussion, as if we were debating the finer points of political theory or the merits of two insurance policies. From time to time we should ask ourselves what we mean when we speak of 'loving God'. Are we crazy about him, besotted with him, in love with him? If we claim to have (or aspire to having) a 'passionate' faith, does that mean that it stirs us physically as well as mentally—and is it reasonable, after all, to talk as if body and mind are properly divisible?

The idea of 'surrendering' to God is common enough, but, instead of thinking in terms of, say, defeat in battle, we can ponder the fact that the idea of surrender, a voluntary self-disarming, is also at the heart of loving physical intimacy. We surrender to the one we love because we are prepared to trust them absolutely, with every single part of who we are; it is only in the context of such absolute trust that true intimacy can flourish and hope to endure. Love should not involve defeat of the other, the powerful overriding the weaker to get their own way and gratify their own desires. That is not love. At best, it is only a pale parody of love; at worst, it is the cruellest abuse. The God we serve and seek to know better is not out to conquer us, forcing us to a grim acknowledgment of our subject status; he courts our hearts gently, longing to coax our love to grow in response to his, that love which is poured out endlessly, beyond any human measure.

## For reflection

'Love sets our hearts on fire and provides meaning, purpose and new identity. It is the most precious commodity among human beings and in creation because love—and love alone—redeems a fallen world. Perhaps this is why, when love goes wrong, the consequences can be of demonic proportions.'

ANDREW CLITHEROW, *DESIRE, LOVE AND THE RULE OF ST BENEDICT*

# 8
## She cheated on him

This is the point where we expect the story to draw to a heart-warming close as the credits roll over the final scene. Perhaps a white horse gallops over the hills and into the sunset, carrying the newly united companions to a wonderful future together. Or maybe—if we're going for a more contemporary feel—a transatlantic plane lifts from the runway, heading for the furthest horizon and carrying our hero and heroine off to all that tomorrow holds for them. This is, emphatically, the script of so many romances, the final tableau of the average fairy tale.

What we are following here, though, is a very different and uncompromisingly harsh story. Realistic? Well, it presents a version of the kind of 'realistic' stories that tend to characterise the bleaker soap operas or a film that would very definitely fall into the 'adult' category. Warning: we're talking more than a touch of 'feel bad' rather than 'feel good'; we're talking betrayal, rejection, bitterness, brokenness and loss.

So, as we continue to hear what happens, we may feel as if thunderclouds have stealthily built up until suddenly they are blotting out the sun. It's as if we are out for a sunny walk in the hills when we look up and see that a catastrophic storm is threatening. The air turns chilly and an ominous, squally wind begins to blow. Disaster is coming and it is too late to do anything about it.

Listen with me and, if you find tears coming, let them come...

When did things begin to change? Later, when he was discovering just how much the phrase 'worst nightmare' could encompass, he would go over those early months and years again and again, searching his memories to see if he could identify the point when their shared life started to unravel. Maybe he had affirmed her too much and too uncritically. Had he spent too much money indulging her whims? Been too quick to change so many aspects of his life to fit in with her plans and agendas? But wasn't that what a loving husband was supposed to do? Lying alone and awake night after night, watching the clock and wondering if and when she would come home, he would torture himself by replaying some of the key moments of rejection. Perhaps this time he would work out exactly what had gone wrong.

Excruciatingly, he could hear her voice so clearly in his head—the same voice that had made the usual marriage promises not so long ago (according to modern-day marriage survival rates, anyway). Now her voice echoed and re-echoed in his head with very different declarations: 'I don't want what you want... I don't care what you think... I don't want you any more... You can't possibly fulfil me... I'm going and you can't stop me...'

He was staggered to realise quite how many kinds of betrayal there were. She betrayed him with other people, not just physically but emotionally, giving away what should have been kept for the two of them alone. She betrayed him by ruthlessly going her own way in life, regardless of his pathetic (even to his own ears) pleas for her to take his feelings into account, just sometimes. It wasn't that he felt used by her so much as completely emptied out by what she had taken from him. She had sucked out from him all the love, all the passion, all the desire, and fed off them to make herself invincibly strong, able to survive and thrive without him—what was left of him, that is.

When he tried to reason with her, she would first mock him and then accuse him of sounding as if he did not want her to be strong, successful and popular. Clearly he had a problem with confident women—was that it? How dare he be so impossibly jealous? Didn't he believe her when she said she was still committed to the relationship? Why would he never take her at her word? When he finally felt he had no choice but to confront her with evidence of her betrayals, she turned on him with volcanic anger. She left the house late that night and he didn't hear from her for four days.

Occasionally, when she would return and condescend to share the marriage bed again for a while, he would wake before dawn and just lie there, looking at her as the light slowly grew. He would imagine that somehow, this time, she would wake and they would have magically found their way back to 'before'. She would smile at him in the old way, mouth and eyes full of warmth and affection; she would reach out and take his hand, and so the new day would begin, both of them finding themselves free to start everything over again.

In his dreams...

But you trusted in your beauty, and played the whore because of your fame, and lavished your whorings on any passer-by. You took some of your garments, and made for yourself colourful shrines, and on them played the whore... You also took your beautiful jewels of my gold and my silver that I had given you, and made for yourself male images, and with them played the whore; and you took your embroidered garments to cover them, and set my oil and my incense before them... You took your sons and your daughters, whom you had borne to me, and these you sacrificed to them to be devoured...

> And in all your abominations and your whorings you did not remember the days of your youth, when you were naked and bare, flailing about in your blood.
> EZEKIEL 16:15–22 (ABRIDGED)

Thus we see how God's loving choice of the unloved foundling that is 'Jerusalem', his care of her and delight in her, opens the way not only for the deepest sharing and vulnerability but also for the worst imaginable pain and rejection. The prophet emphasises the cruelty of the betrayal: Jerusalem was not forced to cheat on her consort through any kind of poverty. In contemporary terms, she was not driven to prostitution so that she could finance her heroin habit or because she had been enslaved through human trafficking; her betrayals were freely chosen, not forced. She is indiscriminate, too, hooking up with any passerby who takes her fancy, a luxury denied to the average 'working girl'. She is described as wealthy, famous and beautiful but she is also stone-hearted, even callously using the gifts showered on her by her lover to further her own promiscuous agendas.

We are reminded how unwanted, neglected and helpless she was 'in the days of [her] youth'; it was her husband's kindness and care that gifted her with beauty and confidence. She is not lacking in self-esteem (the need to boost self-esteem being an all-too-common excuse for all manner of behaviour these days). As far as Jerusalem is concerned, confidence has been corrupted into arrogance, and the generosity shown to her has generated a response not of gratitude but of greed. She wants more and more and more, despite everything she has been given. Rather than trusting her lover to continue to look after her and rather than being willing to explore with him how to handle the desires consuming her, she goes her own way and seeks satisfaction without scruple.

It may be hard to pin down at what point a legitimate hunger develops into greed. Of course, if we are too quick to label our desires 'greed', we fall into the error of simply condemning ourselves without trying to understand what and why we are actually craving. The biblical message is clear, however, and enshrined not least in the Ten Commandments: we should not set our hearts on what belongs to others, whether people or material possessions. Chances are, unless we reflect on what might be fuelling our hunger, we may get what we craved and then find that the wanting continues. Jerusalem's hunger—or greed—proves in just this way to be insatiable.

Having said all this, given our society and, sadly, the Church's historic tendency to denigrate women and heap condemnation on any branded as 'fallen' or 'wanton', we feel uncomfortable agreeing with the prophet's cries of condemnation, joining in and pointing the finger at a 'wicked sinner'. After all, didn't Jesus rebuke such behaviour? We may want to excuse Jerusalem somehow, find ways to understand the choices she made. Perhaps she didn't feel cherished enough. Perhaps her foundling origins left her with a love deficit. Maybe she craved simple affection rather than fine clothes. Ezekiel's story is uncompromising, though, and the pornographic imagery of the original Hebrew in this chapter could be rendered more harshly and crudely than most translators have felt free to do (especially later verses about the spectacular physique of Jerusalem's Egyptian lovers). Transgression is heaped on transgression until it is almost unbearable to read. What kind of Gothic nightmare is this? We are told that Jerusalem even sacrificed the children born of the marriage she betrayed.

This is a very dark and depressing chapter, but it faithfully mirrors the long chain of events that led to the unravelling of God's covenant with Israel and, eventually, to the catastrophe of exile. The exploits of Jerusalem in the prophet's story echo the nation's constant straying (over hundreds of years and despite repeated pleadings, warnings and interventions) after other gods and the fertility cults that presumably seemed to offer a better way of ensuring a good harvest than the laws of their own God. It is very uncomfortable reading, but, if we shy away from the full-frontal shock of its message, we are in danger of developing a partial, even saccharine view of scripture. Yes, the Bible undeniably contains much to reassure, console, guide and inspire us, yet the flipside of God's immense love is his pain and anger when we reject that love. If God did not love us, he would not care what we did to others or to ourselves, whether we chose the way of life or the way of death.

Unconditional love has to carry within it the readiness to risk a broken heart. More than that, to be truly without conditions or limits, it involves the willingness to forgive many times over. And is it possible to calculate what constitutes too great a price to pay for preserving a relationship? How much hurt can we reasonably expect any love, human or heavenly, to withstand? As the story will go on to tell, the depth of the hurt is not to be denied, even by the Lord Almighty.

### For reflection

'The more sinister aspect of greed is its ability to sedate and extinguish desire. It destroys the natural innocence of desire, diminishes its horizons and replaces them with a driven and atrophied possessiveness.'

JOHN O'DONOHUE, *ANAM CARA*

# 9
## She enraged him

Perhaps we should stop now. The story has become too nightmarish and we ought to interrupt the storyteller: 'Enough! Let the man feel able to walk away; let the woman get over herself and calm down. No more heartbreak—time for something to cheer us up.' We can get up from where we have been sitting and scan the library shelves in search of another story. No more grim fairytales but a pleasant modern-day version where the wolf has supper with (and not of) the three little pigs; where Snow White and her stepmother bond through family therapy.

Storytellers have a choice: whether or not they came up with the narrative in the first place, they can adapt it to spare the feelings of their listeners. Sinners can be let off with a warning not to do it again; the sinned-against can have as much tea and sympathy as they want as they come to terms with the changes in their lives. Either way, we are spared the horror of witnessing the consequences of what has been happening.

OK?

Not OK.

Whether we respond to catastrophe with brave words like 'I forgive you' or whether we scream, 'I hope you rot in hell', we still have to endure the consequences of that catastrophe. If we are betrayed, we suffer the effects of that betrayal, even if we assure everybody that it's a relief, in a way, to get things out in the open. However much we long for it, we cannot fast-forward to the aftermath, when all is said and done and the mess is swept away. We can stave off the pain for a time with a chemically induced numbness, but it lies in wait for us.

This is a story of great pain, but listen with me, if you can bear it...

What to do? He walked the streets of the town until he couldn't bear any more sympathetic smiles from old friends. Then he walked the roads leading out into the surrounding fields, oblivious to rain, wind, sun. As he walked, he turned over the options in his mind. He wondered about writing her a letter, setting out his feelings. So he tried it, and cried over it when she sent it back shredded.

Suicide? Something within him resisted the idea of never hearing the end of the story, however many more horrors would have to be faced. His life felt very precious even as he struggled with its disintegration.

Separation and divorce? 'But I still love her,' he whispered as he passed the greasy spoon café where they used to laugh together over a fried breakfast. 'I still love her,' he sighed to himself as he stood on the hill-top where they would some-times come to watch the sunset.

He loved her, but also coming inexorably to the surface was an enormous rage. 'I will not be walked over,' he muttered, clearing the fridge of food that had decayed because he could not eat. Then, at last, the answer to his question came to him. He knew what to do.

Shamelessly, he stole her mobile phone the next time she called by to throw some clothes in the washing machine. He watched her ransack the house in search of it, waited until she had driven off in a temper, and then set to work. As the responses buzzed back, he was amazed at the quantity.

She seemed to be juggling two or three affairs at once, not to mention casual contacts who sounded more than pleased to get the invitation: '8pm fri u n me at my place—park down st'. Then he sent her an email inviting her for a 'really important chat to sort financial stuff'. He knew she wouldn't be able to resist that.

Friday evening came and so did his unusual guests. Many were strangers but some were aghast to find him at the front door. Their good-time mate and drinking buddy—how they must have despised him as they took his wife. His rage burned at a steady white heat, turning his leaden heart to molten metal, ready to sear its way through everything it touched. He looked at his watch; she was due any moment. Then the doorbell rang and at last he was able to usher her inside.

Bolting the front door so that she could not make a quick escape that way, he took her arm and propelled her, none too gently, into the lounge. She looked at the room, packed with anxious, increasingly angry people, and she looked at him. For the first time in... how long? he saw a flicker of self-doubt in her eyes.

Then, as the old but useful cliché goes, all hell broke loose.

Because your lust was poured out and your nakedness uncovered in your whoring with your lovers, and because of all your abominable idols, and because of the blood of your children that you gave to them, therefore, I will gather all your lovers, with whom you took pleasure, all those you loved and all those you hated; I will gather them against you from all around, and will uncover your nakedness to them... I will deliver you into their hands... They shall burn your houses and execute many judgments on you in the sight of many women;

I will stop you from playing the whore... So I will satisfy my
fury on you, and my jealousy shall turn away from you; I will
be calm, and will be angry no longer... I will remember my
covenant with you in the days of your youth, and I will establish
with you an everlasting covenant.

EZEKIEL 16:36–42, 60 (ABRIDGED)

So Jerusalem faces the consequences of her greedy and self-
ish choices. Whether she chose freely (as we are told she did)
or whether we would rather find a deeper cause to explain
how she was driven to such behaviour, she pays a very high
price. What she has done now costs her everything.

The emotional and physical violence described in this
passage makes it uncomfortable reading. Even though there is
no doubt about the extent of the wrongs Jerusalem has done,
not only the grace agenda of the New Testament but present-
day awareness of women's oppression around the world spurs
us to respond with forgiveness, not condemnation. Public
shaming and punishment of the severest kind are the stuff of
today's campaigning headlines: 'Worldwide outcry as woman
sentenced to forty lashes'; 'Global criticism for state execution
of woman by stoning'. It provokes memories of the humiliations
heaped on women who were accused of collaboration with
the enemy during World War II. Accordingly, it seems beyond
belief to find God, even in his anger, sentencing his consort to
such harsh treatment.

The extent of her betrayals is laid bare before a host of
witnesses, but that is only the prelude to far worse treatment.
The prophet tells of stripping, despoliation and all kinds of
abuse. Instead of the tender act of 'covering' which signified
marriage, Jerusalem's nakedness is cruelly exposed, leaving
her as defenceless as when she lay in the field years before as

an abandoned baby. Naked, she is delivered into the hands of a mob of angry men, the implications of which are unbearable to contemplate.

We may wonder whether we dare say of this chapter, 'This is the word of the Lord' and respond, 'Thanks be to God.' Perhaps we struggle to discern any connection between the narrator and the God in whom Christians believe. So what can we possibly do in terms of understanding and learning from this story, given that it is presented as part of scripture?

We reflected previously on the danger of ending up with a saccharine view of the Bible, seeing it as no more than an anthology of heart-warming thoughts and gentle wisdom. I would suggest that what we have in this agonising chapter is neither a legal code nor a mandate for no-holds-barred retribution. Instead it is a brutally honest presentation of the raw emotions of a betrayed lover, putting in the strongest possible terms, 'This is how your actions have made me feel.' And if we would rather tell ourselves that such a response is not true to life—not here and now, anyway—think of those who murder their partners when faced with the truth of their infidelity or who take their young children and die with them, rather than lose them as their family splinters apart.

We may feel more at ease with a faith consisting of warm fuzzies and dreams of a better life in the sweet by-and-by, but it can be curiously consoling to discover that within the discourse of scripture is blistering rage and lacerating pain as well as comfort and joy—and not just in the Psalms. Otherwise, when times of rage and pain come for us (and we can be sure that they will come at some point in our lives), we may feel cut off from God. After all, how could a loving God understand our raging, pain-racked state? Well...

God's overwhelming grief at the breaking of the covenant

relationship must always be held within the bigger picture of his everlasting, unconditional love. God is love, we are told, but love by itself, without relationship, remains unrequited. Anybody who has ever been unrequitedly in love will testify to how torturous it feels. His presence pervades creation, and he longs for us to look up from our own tiny concerns and be alert to his love and all that he would do and be for us—but he will never force us to do so.

Given that he loves and desires us, though, how dare we embark on covenant, on relationship with him, when we will certainly fail to keep our side of it? Perhaps we worry about whether we can bring ourselves to risk disappointing him with our hopelessly flawed humanity. In our weakness and brokenness, we cannot shake off the sense that disappointing others, let alone God, is what we were born to do.

Herein lies the paradox of God's love: his love is unconditional, but relationship at whatever level of intimacy, whether between parent and child, between two adults or between an individual and God, has to involve conditions in order to safeguard the mutual vulnerability involved. We already know that we fail to meet the conditions of a relationship with God, but we also know that we cannot survive the consequences of this failure. So what can the Lover of creation possibly do to connect with his creatures? The extraordinary answer is that he offers his own Son, his own self, to suffer those consequences, which prove to be torment followed by death.

But God's love is stronger than death—any kind of death—as the events of Easter morning prove (and we will come there in due course). At the end of the sad story of Jerusalem and her God, we have the promise of another chance, despite everything that has happened. He will establish an 'everlasting covenant', one that cannot be broken by human failure, and today we live still in the extraordinary light of that new and everlasting covenant.

## For reflection
'The consuming fire of crucified Love is both redemption and judgement; the two are inseparable and indistinguishable.'

HANS URS VON BALTHASAR, *PRAYER*

# 10
## But still he loves

Now the light is fading and each bay of the library holds the glow of a lamp. Our story has nearly finished; the storm of anger has burst, bringing thunderclaps and flash-floods, but at last it is over. Time to survey the debris.

When the turn of life's events leaves us with a pile of rubble which was once a home, a family, a career, we may want to abandon hope altogether. The prospect is not so much renovating a dilapidated cottage as building one from scratch, with the disadvantage of working on ground that is lumpy with broken bits of what stood there before. The task looks impossible, but what choice do we have? We could sit and cry in the ruins but, after a time, even crying becomes too much effort. We struggle to imagine that we might ever have the energy, let alone the vision, to contemplate making anything new.

This is when it is good to remember that there is no blueprint for how life is supposed to be, no monolithic plan, such that if we depart from it we will for ever be stuck in a second-rate scenario. Then again, we cannot hang on to any illusions of seamlessly moving on, airbrushing disaster out of our history.

But there is always hope.

There is always hope—although it may not come in the form we expect.

Holding on to that possibility of hope, we need to listen to the final part of our story. It will take a turn for the better, I promise.

It was an unearthly hour of the night: 3am? 4am? Just the two of them left in the room, metaphorical blood on the carpet. His wife lay on the sofa, humiliated, disgraced, a litter of used tissues around her, eyes swollen with crying, face streaked with mascara. He sat across from her, staring at the spiralling pattern of the Moroccan silk rug, their first anniversary present to each other.

Everything was broken; they were both broken. As he looked at her, broken and quite unbeautiful, he knew that he still loved her, but he could not believe there was the slightest chance that she would ever love him again—if indeed she ever had, deep down.

She stirred, sighed, spoke so hesitantly, so changed from her old manner, that for a moment he wondered if he was imagining it. 'I don't expect you will ever forgive me.'

He counted seven heartbeats before he replied. 'Do you want to be forgiven?' He couldn't bring himself—yet—to ask if she was sorry.

Another long pause and then one word. 'Yes.'

More time passed; neither of them moved or spoke. When he finally looked up, he found that she had been watching him. As their eyes met, he felt the tiniest shock of recognition, a fragmentary half-memory of that long-ago encounter in the garden, when he first realised how his feelings towards her had changed.

She spoke again, a fraction louder. 'I can't think of any reason why you might want to forgive me.'

He did not say anything in response; instead he got up, a little stiffly after hours in more or less the same position, took a DVD from the bookshelf and loaded it into the machine. He pressed 'Play' and the television re-ran for them the story of their wedding day, from the arrival of the flowers at the bride's house to the final leave-taking. It wasn't much of an answer to her statement, not really, but he wanted to show her that he still felt there was something there, a bond between them, something worth trying to retrieve.

Freeze-frame.

Do they stand a chance? Not of rewinding to that wedding day as if nothing has happened since, but of repairing what has been so completely wrecked? The trouble is, even if hope is invoked and promises remade, we are merely human and scars may remain to hinder the free flow of human trust and love. Perhaps we dream of somehow escaping into a parallel life, the tectonic plates of time shifting so that we can return to a point where important choices are still unmade and we can have another go, mindful of the dangerous bends in the road ahead. Whatever we dream, though, the only way is forward, step by step, day by day, waiting for the pain to diminish and at the same time being prepared for the realisation that some scars will never quite heal, not in this life anyway.

Is there a happy ending for our story? Well, it is the storyteller's privilege to fast-forward to the far future. Maybe that is unrealistic, but it would be nice to know what might have happened...

Believe it or not, 30 years have passed. Some of them have been hard years but, especially as time has gone on, mostly good. They have stayed together and now they stand together, the man and the no-longer-young woman, on the hill-top where they still go to watch the sunset on fine evenings. He is stooped now, nearly 80 to her nearly 60, but still strong enough to enjoy the walk. They hold hands, as they always do these days, and each of them also holds the hand of a child, their grandchildren. The sun has slowly dipped below the horizon in a spectacular display of red and gold, while on the other side of the sky a harvest moon is climbing. In that glimmering yellow light they turn and walk home, the four of them.

The end—sort of.

Then I saw a new heaven and a new earth; for the first heaven and the first earth had passed away... And I saw the holy city, the new Jerusalem, coming down out of heaven from God, prepared as a bride adorned for her husband. And I heard a loud voice from the throne saying, 'See, the home of God is among mortals. He will dwell with them; they will be his peoples, and God himself will be with them; he will wipe every tear from their eyes. Death will be no more; mourning and crying and pain will be no more, for the first things have passed away.' And the one who was seated on the throne said, 'See, I am making all things new.'

REVELATION 21:1–5 (ABRIDGED)

Here is the culmination of history, fast-forwarded for our benefit by the prophet John, whose visions unfolded in exile on a Greek island. It is a reiteration of the hope of eventual healing of the whole cosmos, a hope that reverberates throughout scripture, a promise that at the very end of all things is not annihilation, not silence and dust, but a miraculous act of re-creation. 'I am making all things new,' says the one on the throne, and the nuance of the Greek word is not replacement as much as renewal. God's heart always yearns towards restoration, picking up the pieces and making good. However marred and broken we feel, he will not discard us as useless but will set to work to repair us. One day, then, we will be as he always intended us to be, if not in this world, then in the next.

This passage gives us a glimpse of the 'new' Jerusalem. God did not give up on his wayward wife; wonderfully, he continued to forgive and offer ways of rebuilding the relationship. With every excuse to do so, he refused to abandon her as unfit for purpose or trade her in for a better model. And here she is, once again a beautiful bride as she was always meant to be, as radiant as if none of the other stuff had ever happened—which, as far as God is concerned, is in fact the case.

Truly, all things are being made new.

The blessed reality, as presented here by John, is that rather than wishing for a magic door so that we can go back and unpick our mistakes, we can continue our journey in the God-given confidence that a future day will come when our knots will be untangled, our messes sorted out, and our nagging injuries finally made better.

The promise is that God can and will surely bring life out of death. Of course, this does not mean that we wilfully choose the way of death instead of life; as we have seen, we must live with the consequences of our choices, however much we regret them. What it does mean is that, quite simply, the bottom line is redemptive resurrection love. It is this love that lies above, beyond, beneath and behind everything—inescapable.

Do we ever think about the greatness of God's love and desire for us? Or do we hide behind a carapace of excuses—how useless we are; how we don't pray enough, worship enough, care enough, love enough in return? Focusing on our failings is hardly an inducement to embark on relationship. I wonder whether it amuses or saddens God to hear us whine, 'I'm no good... you wouldn't want to bother with me... I'm really not up to it.' Sadly, we may come to believe in our own miserable monologue so thoroughly that we refuse even to acknowledge the presence of our Lover.

However much we think we can shield ourselves from such enormous love, such powerful desire for response, we will find it reaching through the smallest chink in our scrappy personal defences and touching our hearts with a gentle finger. This may happen through the simplest gesture of kindness from another person, through a soul-stirring sermon by a famous preacher, as we hold out our hands to receive the bread and wine of Holy Communion, or as we take a moment to stand in the first warm sunshine of the year and relish its touch on our faces.

We are invited to live in the hope that, in the end, the universe will not simply collapse in on itself, shrinking into a void. Instead, it will be infinitely enlarged until there is room for the infinite Creator to enter and live face to face with his people. Once, long ago, he reduced himself to a single human cell, incarnate of the virgin Mary and made man; one day, all that we understand of time and space will be turned inside-out as the kingdom of heaven and the kingdom of this world are finally and visibly united. The work of love will be complete—or, perhaps, complete in the sense of foundations having been finished, so that the work of transformation and healing can continue for ever.

With that thought, our time in the library is finished; we need to go and explore more of this safe house. Maybe we venture out into the corridor in trepidation, still musing on what we have heard, or maybe we have had enough of stories and want some action. Either way, as we emerge, we are pulled up short because a woman is waiting for us, perched on a cushioned window-seat.

We would probably describe her as 'older', but her alert eyes and ease of movement as she rises to her feet do not suggest imminent decrepitude. Her face is kind but at the same time watchful, as if very little by way of human meanness or deceit or cruelty would come as a surprise.

'Come with me,' she says, and her voice is as kind as her face but with an edge of authority. 'There are people for you to meet.'

## For reflection

'No one is unaffected by unconditional love. If someone has loved us completely and unshakeably, we must be changed. We live the rest of our lives knowing that we can be, have been, wholly lovable. Love buries itself in our hearts; it works on us; it makes it impossible for us not to believe in love and—believing in it—we will always, eventually, express it in our lives.'

TERESA MORGAN, SEASONS OF THE SPIRIT

Part Three

# Love and loss

# 11
# The mother: love

The woman is our guide as we walk along the corridor, up a staircase, along another corridor and up a further staircase that brings us to what appears to be the top floor of the house. We reach a narrow landing and ahead is a doorway leading to a long, dimly lit room. At the far end, people are sitting round a low table, talking and laughing quietly together. As we cross the threshold, the warm, drowsy air of the room envelops us. The walls have been painted dark red and are crowded with pictures—paintings, framed photographs, maps—and comfortable armchairs and sofas are arranged across the carpeted floor.

'Have a seat, where you can find one. This is a good place for resting. Resting and reflecting. Remembering, too, if you like.' The woman smiles but her eyes are thoughtful as she looks at us.

Remembering: what might we possibly want to remember from before? The snarling aggression in the city streets, the roaring traffic, the loneliness?

'Anything you want…' she goes on, as if replying to a question, still surveying us carefully. 'Just a thought, though —the more you remember something, the more you bring back the feelings to do with it, the good but also the bad. And some of the bad can be hard to bear, even after a lot of time has passed.

'You see,' she continues, after another moment of reflective silence, 'there is not a single person who does not have memories they treasure but also ones that torment them.

And they will have memories that they return to, again and again, to try and understand. What was going on? Why did that happen? What did it all mean? Maybe they imagine that by replaying a scene over and over in their head, the faces and words and gestures will suddenly fall into a pattern that makes sense of everything that happened before and afterwards.'

There is another pause. The people at the far end of the room have fallen quiet now, listening to what the woman is saying.

'You know,' she goes on at last, 'remembering can be very precious because it can bring back something or someone we thought we had lost. As we remember that thing or that person, old, tender feelings can live again, as if no time has passed, as if nothing else has happened. And, sometimes, that is what we need to give us the strength to walk on.'

She walks over to a wooden sideboard, ranged against the dark red wall, and picks up a photo frame.

'Look.' She holds it out towards us—a digital photo display, flashing up a succession of images of a beautiful dark-haired young woman holding a baby, a toddler, a grinning little boy. As we view scene after scene, the rapturous love between them, the delight of mother in son and devotion of son to mother, dazzles: the two of them on the beach, laughing in the rain, dancing, hugging, asleep in each other's arms. Looking at such images, it is hard not to smile, and the woman is also smiling as she looks at them, this time without any reserve in her face.

'Some of you will know,' she says, shaking her head, still smiling. 'There is nothing quite like it—the firstborn, especially if you have longed for that baby's coming, month after month, before you even conceived. And although you know it must happen, it is still a shock when something male comes out of your body. Of course you know it happens, but it still seems the strangest thing when it happens to you! And then that little boy grows into a man, taller and stronger than you, and you look at him and still remember how he once fitted into your lap, top to toe on your knees.

'You look at him, grown, and you know for sure that he is the most handsome, most wonderful son ever born, because he is yours. There is no one else like him in the whole world and never will be again. He is irreplaceable, always.'

She puts down the photo frame, the smile lingering at the corners of her mouth, and when she looks at us again, her gaze is like sunlight. 'Whatever some people may say, I for one think the love is worth any loss.'

The angel Gabriel was sent by God to a town in Galilee called Nazareth, to a virgin engaged to a man whose name was Joseph... The virgin's name was Mary. And he came to her and said, 'Greetings, favoured one! The Lord is with you.' But she was much perplexed by his words and pondered what sort of greeting this might be. The angel said to her, 'Do not be afraid, Mary, for you have found favour with God. And now, you will conceive in your womb and bear a son, and you will name him Jesus...' Mary said to the angel, 'How can this be, since I am a virgin?' The angel said to her, 'The Holy Spirit will come upon you, and the power of the Most High will overshadow you; therefore the child to be born will be holy; he will be called Son of God...' Then Mary said, 'Here am I, the servant of the Lord; let it be with me according to your word.'
LUKE 1:26–38 (ABRIDGED)

How can we possibly get to grips with this Bible passage, this beyond-extraordinary encounter? All artists, writers, story-tellers and preachers ought to falter here and admit that, in the end, they can only come up with the vaguest of vague impressions, a hopelessly limited 'something like'. Should we imagine the modest recoil of a Raphael virgin, the uncertainty of a Rossetti (go on, look them up online), the stylised pose of an Orthodox icon, or something more homely—a teenage girl in Middle Eastern first-century peasant dress, dropping her water jug as she is startled at the well?

In struggling to understand what happened and what it meant, perhaps we can think of a moment when we felt chosen in some way, as if a hand had reached into our lives, taken hold of us and brought about profound change. If we think long enough, we may be able to call to mind such a point in time (happening to others, if not to us), a pivotal event after which things were never quite the same again.

Why me—or you? Why not me—or you?

God knows the answer to such questions.

Let's stop and try to reason out why the Son of God did not follow 'divine convention' for his incarnation. In line with the sort of stories told by many of the world's cultures and faiths, he could have chosen to spring fully grown from a suitably suggestive cleft in a sacred mountain or gallop down from heaven on the back of a white elephant. It would surely have been no problem for the Father to shape the Son from a handful of desert sand or even bring him to life—why not?—from a pile of autumn leaves. Instead, Mary was chosen, singled out for all time from every other woman who ever had been or ever would be, chosen as God-Bearer.

There was a father too, of course—Joseph, the role model for fathers everywhere who have had to care for a child not their own. Yet this unusually special son could easily have been a foundling, discovered in a special place after words of special prophecy. He could have been delivered in the arms of an angel, fully formed, to his waiting foster home. But it seems that Jesus needed a birth-mother. He had to be born of a woman, actually partaking of her flesh and blood, nurtured inside her body, suckled by her body, held in her arms, kissed by her, loved.

Why?

It was so, surely, because that gestation, those nine months in a woman's body, and that prosaically natural birth in some mysterious way accelerated the process of redemption, the process that culminated at Calvary and beyond. God himself is born as human, literally embodying salvation. At the point of conception (and it is interesting to speculate whether this happened while the angel was speaking to her, or whether she was already pregnant, or whether she sensed it happening later), God and the image of God merge into one. The incarnation did not happen as a necessary, essentially time-wasting prelude to the crucifixion; it was a bestowing of blessing and divine favour on the world that God had made, on the people created to bear his likeness.

Thus everything, absolutely everything, changes. The realms of time and eternity collide; the furthest parameters of possibility are redrawn to encompass the infinite. But at that pivotal moment of angelic encounter, what we actually see is a young woman standing in bright Middle Eastern sunlight, saying, 'Here am I, the servant of the Lord; let it be with me according to your word.' In that response, accepting with immeasurable grace her status as chosen one, she is herself eternally transfigured, made over into the new Eve for the redeemed creation.

As we look at the new Eve, with the Son of the Most High in her arms, we see a girl cradling her firstborn son, Saviour of the world but none the less her own baby boy. Just as humanity is hallowed by the Creator's choice to humble himself to the status of creature, so the love of a mother for her child is hallowed because God himself partook of it. Considered logically, it would have been much simpler for Jesus to burst on to the scene as an adult, perhaps a wandering preacher appearing from over the sea or out of the wilderness. Being labelled 'the carpenter's son' did not do much for his Messiahship credentials. Even so, for 30 years he lived in his family home, surrounded by his mother's love and care.

Maybe in those quiet 30 years, the Son of God simply enjoyed being loved, with the kind of instinctive love, motherly love, that means the one who loves is prepared to die for the beloved without a second's hesitation, that means she sees beauty and intelligence, potential and achievement, in the beloved where outsiders may struggle to discern anything particularly special. Mary was not chosen as an 'empty vessel', a mere incubator for the divine embryo; she was chosen as his mother. She loved her son and, in loving him, she (like mothers everywhere and across time) thereby taught him something of what love means and what it means to love.

## For reflection

'God loves as mothers love—extravagantly, pouring love out without measure. God loves intimately, each one of us as a different person, and equally, every one of us as much as all the others, however many there are.'

Teresa Morgan, *Seasons of the Spirit*

# 12
# The friends: love

In the soothing atmosphere of this attic room, remembering starts to feel less risky. When the very air is imbued with safety, we sense that this is somewhere we can truly relax. Here we can think about unpacking (or at least venturing near) some of those memories boxed and stored in the darkest, most spidery corner of our selves. Here, instinct tells us, there will be arms to hold us, if that is what we want, and kindness that is unembarrassed by the free flow of tears.

Not in the mood for tears? No problem.

Let's venture down the room to where the group is seated round the table. These people have been eating and drinking together, enjoying an Indian takeaway and a few bottles of beer, by the looks of things. From the casual intimacy of bodies resting against each other, arms draped around shoulders, it is clear that this is a group of close and trusted friends, both men and women, and so familiar and at ease with one another that they are free of the petty undercurrents of rivalry and flickers of sexual tension that can test the bonds of so many such groups.

As we hesitate on the edge, unsure whether they will welcome company, they notice our presence, they smile, and the circle widens far enough to make room for us. Conversation continues to flow between them and it is clearly up to us to listen and learn when it is appropriate to join in, rather than expecting attention to shift to us.

As we pick up the thread of their talk, it becomes clear that they are remembering together, creating a composite picture out of their shared memories. This picture is illuminated by the love with which they speak, until it is almost as if the one they recall is visibly projected in miniature on the table in the middle of them, a hologram beamed by the heart.

'I used to hope that I was the one closest to him.' It is one of the women speaking. In the dim light of this long room, she looks young-ish, pretty-ish. Her voice sounds young anyway, if a little tired and wistful.

The slightly older woman next to her runs a soothing hand along her friend's arm. 'I think there were times when each of us hoped that.'

'But…'—a man with a straggly, rather half-hearted beard leans across the table towards them to emphasise his point. 'He definitely needed all of us, at different times and in different ways.'

'He needed his own space, too.' The man who speaks now is slighter and his voice much harder to catch than his bearded neighbour's. 'Don't you think he kept a space round him that none of us was allowed into?'

'I used to worry that he might be lonely,' the tired and wistful woman says, tiredly and wistfully.

The straggly-bearded man smiles and reaches out to touch her hand. 'Not lonely. I don't think he was ever lonely. Alone, yes, but that's what he wanted. He was totally his own person.'

It is as if that affectionate, undemanding touch unlocks something in her. Abruptly her face crumples and she tries to swallow the beginnings of a sob. 'It wasn't that I wanted him just for myself. I was just so desperate to make sure that he was happy.

'Then again…' She stops and sighs. 'In so many ways it was enough, just being with him, and, when I was not with him, knowing that before long I would be with him again.'

She looks round the circle of kind faces (let us hope that we look kind, too, and not simply puzzled by this curious discussion). 'You know, I can't imagine feeling such a connection with another person again. Even though—' she breaks off again, gulps, regains control. 'Even though I can't be with him now, I will never, ever stop feeling, well, blessed by what I had then, in that connection. I remember, when he looked at me—'

Her composure disintegrates and the circle of friends responds with hugs and soothing noises. Thus it is that we may be the only ones who notice the words of the softly spoken, slightly built man: 'He looked at me like that, too.'

His eyes are shiny with tears, but the memory makes his smile beautiful.

Six days before the Passover Jesus came to Bethany, the home of Lazarus, whom he had raised from the dead. There they gave a dinner for him. Martha served, and Lazarus was one of those at the table with him. Mary took a pound of costly perfume made of pure nard, anointed Jesus' feet, and wiped them with her hair. The house was filled with the fragrance of the perfume.

JOHN 12:1–3

This is one of those Gospel passages that would surely make many people's list of top ten favourite New Testament readings. We see Jesus at ease with his friends and then the lavish anointing, followed by the denunciation of one of the other disciples, shocked by the wanton generosity. As with so many favourite readings, the challenge is how to read it with fresh eyes, to see past a mental tableau of posed figures in quaint costume in a stage-set 'Bible times' home. We can try to imagine it as it would have been, a moment in time when the final outcome of events was unclear, when all kinds of possible futures might have been hovering unspoken in the minds of those present.

We are told elsewhere in the Gospels that Jesus' relationship with his own family was troubled at times, as they struggled to understand what exactly he was up to. Here in Bethany, some two miles from Jerusalem, he could be at rest and receive the love and honour of his three close friends, each expressing that love in their own way. Martha served the guests with food, as was customary for the women of the house; Mary apparently had a tendency to break with convention in an outrageous way. Luke 10:39 records how she once sat with the men to listen to Jesus; here she offers a humiliating and also deeply intimate act of devotion. Only the lowest of the low touched the feet of another; a woman would only uncover and loosen her hair as a sign of love—for her husband—or as a sign of mourning, indicating a total loss of self-respect and dignity in the face of great grief.

Two sisters—one honouring their friend in the traditional way with food and hospitality, the other by a show of love that unforgettably subverted tradition. And their brother—what of Lazarus, identified as one whom Jesus loved, just like 'the beloved disciple' who is so described only in John's Gospel (and traditionally identified as John himself)? It is hard to imagine what could possibly have been going through his mind as he lounged at table with the one who had brought him back from the dead. We can only speculate as to how extraordinary that connection must have been.

Any kind of life-changing event forges links between those involved. The one who saves a life may find that they are bound to the one saved by the latter's debt of gratitude; equally, the one who takes a life is inextricably linked with the one whose life has been taken, and with those left behind to mourn. Whether life-saver or life-taker, that person becomes for ever the pivotal character in a particular drama, without whose intervention everything would have been different.

At the same time, in the person of Jesus we see one who, during his earthly life, did not remain remote from human contact, appearing as *deus ex machina* to dispense wisdom and miracles and then withdrawing into a special heavenly realm. Yes, he needed time apart in the hills to pray, but so do many people. He was not a hermitic figure, like some of the more inscrutable and prickly Desert Fathers, shunning mortal distractions in order to focus as intently as possible on the heavenly realm—or, indeed, like his cousin John, the wild and shaggy desert prophet.

Just as Jesus did not burst into the world fully formed, but was born of a woman and raised by her, thus hallowing a mother's love for her child, so he lived in close and loving relationship with others as an adult. They loved and needed him; he loved and needed them (remember, for instance, his anguish in the garden of Gethsemane, when his friends first fell asleep and then ran off and left him). He hallowed not only the mother–child relationship, as we saw earlier, but also the life-sustaining bonds of friendship—and such friendship means not casual acquaintance or 500-odd 'online friends', but love. We're talking the kind of mutual love where each gives the other what they are able to give, and the other does not selfishly demand what cannot, for whatever reason, be given. It's the kind of love that says, 'We accept each other, look out for each other's interests, welcome each other, strive to understand each other, be there for each other as much as we are able, celebrate our belonging together...' and all this in a way that has the potential to draw in rather than exclude newcomers.

In the context of such relationships, we learn what it truly means to connect with another, not to flatter ourselves ('look who I'm friends with!') but because true connection can bring life, growth and fruitfulness. Freely expressed love, grace and generosity have the power to call forth a corresponding response, as the heaven-sent love, grace and generosity of Jesus warmed those around him and nurtured in them the beginnings of a kinship likeness to him, their friend and brother.

In the context of such relationships, bonds can develop that are strong and grow stronger over time, while remaining flexible enough to last through the harshest of life circumstances. Then, when we meet again, even if it is after many years, the connection is still there, unmistakable.

In the context of such love, many fears can start to be put aside, not least the lurking fear that loss has the last word.

### For reflection

'There is only one love, and that is God, who is present, recognised or not, in every love.'

TIMOTHY RADCLIFFE, *WHAT IS THE POINT OF BEING A CHRISTIAN?*

# 13
# The friends: loss

The group round the table is breaking up now, wandering off in ones and twos. It is unclear whether we should follow or whether we should simply hang around here. The protocol of this house seems to be that people can drift together or apart as they please, finding whatever shared or solitary space they need.

And do we yet know what we really need?

Do we yet know what we really want?

We may envy the easy camaraderie of the group but despair of ever having the time and space to build such relationships. We may crave to be loved as the wise woman clearly loved her child, but it is surely impossible to replicate the depth of the maternal bond.

If we recognise that we are no more than onlookers at the love and security of others, we start to recognise the extent of our emptiness, our lovelessness and our loss. Such recognition can begin to burn inside us, tightening the throat, pricking at the eyes, quickening the heartbeat. Unfortunately, there are no short cuts: we have to understand what we have lost before we can begin to identify what we need, let alone what we want.

That journey may be a fearful one, and, in our growing awareness of loss, building towards despair, we may doubt that we will ever be brave enough to make it.

Take a deep breath; let the despair die down. The challenge we face is, in fact, a relatively small one (although, if our despair is deep, it can still seem overwhelming). All we have to do right now is discover the next step that we have to take. That step may turn out to be the first on the journey that we find so daunting, so fearful, which may turn out to be less daunting and fearful than we expected.

As it happens, two of the group, a couple of older men, have stayed at the table. For some reason we did not notice them before, but now we see that one is clearly troubled. He is talking, almost to himself, in hurried, tense tones, his words stumbling over each other, while his friend sits beside him, listening and making a brief interjection from time to time.

'I never realised that I could be that cruel. I'd always said I could never do that sort of thing, not me, but now I see it was a case of "there but for the grace of God". I know that now. I'm no better—no, actually I'm much, much worse than other people, because I always assumed I was better. I would do anything to be able to go back and change what happened. When I think back to that moment, it's so clear how totally stupid I was. I saw what I expected to see and I never gave any chance for reply, just launched straight in there and now it's too late. It was more than a verbal slap in the face. It was a verbal knife in the heart.'

His friend speaks quietly. 'You don't have to stay locked into the remembering. You've gone over it so many times.'

'But it was all because of love, you see. I loved so much that when I realised I was not going to be loved back in the way that I wanted, my own love actually turned into hate. And, more than anything, I couldn't bear the threat of losing that love, so it was as if something inside me took over and decided to destroy the whole thing. At least that way nobody else could take it.'

'But,' says his friend slowly, 'it sounds as if you forgot that the other person existed outside your own heart, that they had the right to choose how to respond to your love.'

'Yes, I see that now, now that it's too late.'

'One thing has come to an end, that's true. But that does not mean everything is over for you, for ever.'

'What does that possibly mean?' The troubled one sounds angry now. 'Tell me how I can possibly continue on my own, without—'

'Because—maybe you've forgotten this—I've had to face exactly that same choice, and more than once...' The troubled one's troubled words dry up; he looks at his friend, who continues, 'You see, I think you can hold on to the hope that love can come again, that it can somehow regrow in your life, even after the worst losses.'

Now Peter was sitting outside in the courtyard. A servant-girl came to him and said, 'You also were with Jesus the Galilean.' But he denied it... After a little while the bystanders came up and said to Peter, 'Certainly you are also one of them, for your accent betrays you.' Then he began to curse, and he swore an oath, 'I do not know the man!' At that moment the cock crowed. Then Peter remembered what Jesus had said: 'Before the cock crows, you will deny me three times.' And he went out and wept bitterly... When Judas... saw that Jesus was condemned, he repented and brought back the thirty pieces of silver to the chief priests and the elders. He said, 'I have sinned by betraying innocent blood.' ... Throwing down the pieces of silver in the temple, he departed; and he went and hanged himself.

Matthew 26:69–75; 27:3–5 (abridged)

Here we have two dear companions of Jesus, both of whom abandon him to his enemies. One has been a byword for treachery ever since; the other was not only forgiven and reinstated by the risen Jesus himself, but became the 'rock' on whom the Church was built.

Peter fancied himself as brave, yet in some ways he turned out to be weaker than the rest because he failed to acknowledge his weakness. Admittedly, he did stay on after the arrest in Gethsemane, sneaking behind at a safe distance to the high priest's courtyard where the first of Jesus' trials took place. But then, when he is recognised as one of the Galilean's followers, he denies it, and his denials grow in intensity until the terrible moment when he realises he is doing exactly what Jesus had foretold. We might consider his behaviour understandable, given the high tension and terror of the moment, but it still shattered his own sense of who he was and what he was capable of.

According to Matthew's Gospel, Judas seems not to have realised that Jesus' life would be in danger if he fell into the hands of the authorities. With the easy judgment of hind-sight, this sounds extraordinarily naive—yet John the Baptist was initially imprisoned rather than executed, and was only beheaded because of a gruesome plot hatched by Herod's wife. None of the Gospels give any clear reason as to why Judas betrayed Jesus or any indication of the qualities for which Jesus had chosen him as one of the Twelve in the first place. Maybe he felt he was doing Jesus a favour because his arrest would surely lead to no more than a public and rather humiliating reprimand. At worst, he might be imprisoned until the situation cooled down or until he had moderated some of his more immoderate views. Then again, maybe Judas was angry that he was not part of the 'inner circle' of

Peter, Andrew, James and John. Thus he started to distance himself from the others, eventually choosing betrayal as a way of asserting his independence from Jesus and his too-radical teaching.

Too late, so Matthew's Gospel tells us, Judas realises his mistake. He tries to give back the blood money to the religious authorities, and then he takes his own life. We should note, by the way, that the first chapter of the book of Acts tells a different story—that Judas died a particularly nasty accidental death. Either way, his life and apostleship were finished. He was not there to meet the risen Jesus and see that everything had turned out right in the end, just as had been promised.

If we are not honest with ourselves, our love can sometimes start to grow perilously close to hatred. We are not told that Judas hated Jesus, but, if there had been a close relationship between rabbi and disciple, it must have become very twisted and darkened to bring the latter to turn on the former. Sometimes we actually start to hate what we love because we do not feel that our love is given the response it deserves. We turn on somebody—a friend, a relative, a lover—and treat them cruelly because we are angry about the way they make us feel, even though we say (to them and to ourselves) that we love them.

There is an uncomfortable truth wrapped up in this, which circumstances may one day force on our attention: what we imagine to be love turns out, when closely examined, to be a veneer over a deep layer of desperate need. In consequence, we do not see clearly or truthfully the one we say we love; when we look at them, we do not see an individual, one to whom we can give as well as from whom we can receive, so much as a solution to our own emptiness, our weakness, our overwhelming sense of inadequacy.

If circumstances do not lead us to correct our faulty vision, we can end up losing so very, very much more than we expected.

Peter and Judas: two dear companions of Jesus. Both betrayed the love they had for him. One came back to love from loss; the other—was he altogether lost?

We don't know.

Peter was reinstated, despite his shameful actions. Meeting the risen Jesus on the lake shore, he had to remember what he had done, but this was remembering as healing and redemption rather than simply playing and replaying the memory of what had gone wrong. In that remembering, he was set free from the memory of what he had done; he was brought back to walk in the light. Judas, on the other hand, was consumed by remorse and died in the lonely hell of that remorse. He remembered all too clearly and was tortured by that remembering because, as far as he knew—as far as anybody knew between Good Friday and Easter morning— Jesus was dead and gone because of what he had done.

Remorse can be the beginning of healing, however. It can be the sign of a heart still human enough to hurt.

Think of the thief on the cross, the dying man who asked Jesus to remember him and who, in return, was promised a place at the Saviour's side in paradise. Think of the story that Jesus told of the loving father who ran to meet his wayward son while he was still walking along the road that led home.

Think of Mother Julian of Norwich, who, over years of wise reflection, wondered whether anybody could truly be described as beyond the reach of God's saving love. Think, too, of the ancient tradition of the harrowing of hell, the belief that Jesus descended to the depths before his resurrection to retrieve those who had died before they could respond to his redeeming sacrifice.

Dare we imagine that Judas was brought back then, blinking in the light of heaven and weeping with relief as he was swept into the endless embrace of heavenly love?

We don't know—but we can hope.

## For reflection

'The insidious power of good is enough to undermine the whole contraption of evil... Even one doubt of evil allows the grace of God to enter in, and entering to make all things different.'

A.M. ALLCHIN, *THE JOY OF ALL CREATION*

# 14
# The mother: loss

Where now?

Let us wander slowly to the very end of the room, where there is a sash window, uncurtained. If we look through, we will see that, outside, night has fallen. But how strange—the glow of the city should be staining the sky red, yet, from the windows of this house, we look out not at sodium glare but at a brilliant scattering of stars.

As we stare at this puzzlingly perfect night, somebody comes to stand next to us. It is the woman who led us to this room in the first place. In the dim light we cannot see the expression on her face clearly, but her voice is so gentle as she turns to speak to us.

'And you,' she says gently, 'what have you lost—or maybe never found? Do you know yet what it is you really want?'

What dare we say? We can spend our entire lives shying away from those questions, or assuming that we know the correct answers because we have been given them already— by our teachers, our parents, our society, or by the voice of the terrible, insatiable craving inside us, which we have been too scared or confused or plain tired to address or even identify properly.

Can we begin to address it now? Standing in this gentle presence, we sense that here is one who will not judge or be impatient with our fumbling attempts to explain what's wrong. The great fear that we may have to master, though, is that once we start on the process, everything will finally start to fall apart, ourselves included. Best to hold it all together—for now, anyway.

But the woman is speaking again, half to herself, half to us, filling the awkward silence that we have created by not replying to her questions.

'You know,' she says thoughtfully, 'the worst fears are the ones we dare not face. We may fear loss so dreadfully that we never allow ourselves to let go in love, just in case the worst happens. Or we may love so passionately and hungrily that we spend our whole lives afraid of the inevitable loss that must surely come, because isn't loss what always lies ahead of us?'

She pauses, perhaps waiting for a response, but we are not ready to give one, not yet.

'Then,' she goes on slowly, 'the very worst thing happens, the worst that we can possibly imagine, the greatest loss of all, whatever that is. And afterwards we find we cannot bear to be in the present moment, because there is nothing for us in that moment except horrible, aching absence. So we escape to the past, going back and back until we come to the time when we were happiest, when life should have stopped right there, but of course we didn't know what lay ahead. And we can't bear to think about the future even for an instant, because of the lies that have crept into our hearts along with the grief and the loss, telling us that everything was entirely our fault, that we will never, ever feel better again, that now and for ever we are alone in the universe.'

The starlight seems fainter now, the darkness pressing like felt against the uncurtained window. To be alone, in the thickest, most silent and eternal night, alone with the fears that we spend so much energy keeping in check—that is something we dare not contemplate, but somehow it is starting to feel scarily possible. This woman and her gentle words are weakening our resistance, and we fear to speculate what will happen when that crashes down.

'And then,' she says, still gentle, still commanding our attention, 'then at last we may begin to find that although the loss does not change, we do. We cannot regain what is gone or who is gone, or not in the way things were before, but we learn to stop listening to the lies that have entered our hearts. We start to see the possibility of a new kind of wholeness—scarred, perhaps, but also healed. We see that, maybe, what we have started to learn can help lead others from even the deepest loss to the beginnings of recovery, the recovery of love.'

Meanwhile, standing near the cross of Jesus were his mother, and his mother's sister, Mary the wife of Clopas, and Mary Magdalene. When Jesus saw his mother and the disciple whom he loved standing beside her, he said to his mother, 'Woman, here is your son.' Then he said to the disciple, 'Here is your mother.' And from that hour the disciple took her into his own home.
JOHN 19:25–27

Is there a worse pain than burying your own child? What is probably worse is not being able to bury your child, when the beloved body is lost, left behind or taken away, and you have nothing to mourn. That has happened and continues to happen to so many women in times and places of war, turmoil and repression.

While the loss of any child is appalling, losing the firstborn can be a peculiarly acute pain. This is the prototype, the one with whom the mother learnt... well, how to be a mother—the one who set the standard, for good or ill, for any child who came after in the family. The firstborn inevitably carries the weight of parental expectations, the hopes, dreams and fears that emerge to blight or bless the next generation.

So this was the reward of Mary, God-Bearer, for her extravagant offering of herself, body and soul, to the will of heaven. We should not forget the prophetic words of old Simeon in the temple, recorded in Luke's Gospel, as he held the infant Jesus. He spoke of salvation, light and glory, but also warned that there would be uncomfortable revelation even of the secret thoughts of many people and—most forebodingly—a sword piercing the mother's very soul.

The Gospel writers made little or nothing of Mary's presence at the crucifixion of her son, with only John's Gospel mentioning her, in the context of Jesus passing her into the care of 'the disciple whom he loved'. We have to turn to the Church's artistic and devotional heritage to find reflection on the pain of the mother's loss, reflection on the piercing grief foretold by Simeon. Indeed, the tradition of the 'seven sorrows' of Mary identifies seven moments in the Gospel accounts that would have wounded her heart, starting with that encounter with Simeon and ending as the dead body of Jesus was placed in the tomb.

The medieval Latin poem known as *Stabat Mater*, from its opening words, portrays the stark scene at Golgotha, as Jesus hung there dying and his mother stood by, unable to do anything except grieve and watch:

*Stabat mater dolorosa*
*juxta Crucem lacrimosa*
*dum pendebat Filius.*

'*Filius*'—the son. The word falls like a huge weight at the end of the line, exposing the full horror of what is happening. A mother is weeping beside an instrument of torture, and who is nailed there? None other than her own son.

As well as grief, there was the public shame and humiliation of crucifixion. She was the mother of a convicted criminal, sentenced to the worst punishment commonly used at that time. We may have pity, or reflect with fascinated horror, on the mothers of those whose crimes thrust them into the media spotlight: the serial killers, the suicide bombers, the ones branded as inhuman and monstrous for what they have done. Imagine, then, the anguish of the mother who knows that her child is innocent, that a terrible miscarriage of justice has branded him or her as notorious.

In reading the passion narratives, it is so easy to forget that, for those waiting in agony of spirit next to the dying man, this really was the end of their hopes. Any prospect of messianic victory over the occupying forces in the land, of restoration of national peace and prosperity, of the coming of the Day of the Lord—all gone. And for the mother, weeping, there was the special agony of losing her firstborn, her flesh and blood. Whatever else she had hoped for, prayed for and anticipated, it would never, in a thousand years of wildest speculation, have encompassed this dreadful and messy conclusion.

We may wonder if Mary ever looked back to that original moment of annunciation and wondered whether she had made the right choice. When she made her response to the angel, she would surely have had little or no sense of the full immensity and cost of the sacrifice that she would be called to make. 'Here am I, the servant of the Lord; let it be with me according to your word'—and it was so. A child was born; more than 30 years later, he died a terrible death and his mother's heart was torn apart so that the scheme of salvation might be worked out to its conclusion.

When we speak of being 'touched by God', we may not consider how that touch could burn us like fire. Yes, we can imagine the Spirit brushing past us as gently as a dove's wing, but when Isaiah saw the Lord in the temple, a seraph seared his mouth with a live coal from the altar, making him pure for the task of proclamation. We may not feel ready for a touch that scorches or maims us, even if healing and wholeness are the final result. We may not care to remember the words of Jesus about taking up our cross and being prepared to lose our lives in order to follow his way.

As we think of Mary crying by the cross, Lady of Sorrows, we see that we must be prepared for love to demand an apparently impossible sacrifice; we must be willing for it to lead us through brokenness and suffering. We must be willing to receive the strange blessing that is sorrow, because it can, through the grace of God, open us to connect more profoundly with the suffering of the world.

Are we willing?

She was.

## For reflection

'The moment of the annunciation is the moment which makes sense of all other moments... it is a moment in which eternity really has come, in which God is present and at work. Both the birth and death of Jesus witness to the depth and immensity of God's love, and to the infinite openness and potential of human life.'

A.M. ALLCHIN, *THE JOY OF ALL CREATION*

# 15
## The end

As we loiter here, staring out at the very black, very peaceful night sky, we might begin to wonder where our journey can possibly take us now. Perhaps we should go back through this room and wander along some more corridors, find another room and then another and another, meeting more people, listening to more conversations, perhaps joining in some debate or speculation, and eventually drifting away. Or is there another way?

Seeming to sense our thought, the woman speaks again: 'Look...' She points and we look and see what, somehow, we had not seen before.

In the wall to our left, a white door stands slightly ajar. The paintwork is scratched and scruffy, and the entrance rather too narrow for its height, like the door to an attic or a cellar—not one for general public use, anyway. But is a half-open door really an invitation to enter? Especially if we have no idea whether it is right for us to do so, or where it might lead.

Take a step, and a second, and we are on the point of crossing the threshold, and then we hear the woman's voice behind us, one last time: 'Go.' It sounds like a benediction.

Beyond the narrow door is a staircase, winding down and down and down and down. There is enough light to see—just—but where this dingy light comes from is uncertain. As we descend, fingertips brushing the wall for balance (no sign of a health-and-safety handrail), the air grows colder and danker, with a mustiness that lingers at the back of the throat. The light fades steadily until we have to feel for each stair before stepping on to it.

Down, down, down.

When darkness grows, our senses can begin to play tricks on us. Eyes detect pyrotechnic displays of coloured light; the inner ear starts to broadcast a symphony orchestra in full flight or a crashing rock band at high volume. Here, on this long, dreary descent, we find ourselves seeing and hearing things we once knew but have since forgotten about. We may suddenly be confronted with images of events that excited us or numbed us with boredom, places where we have found peace or disturbance, memories of how we loved or hated. If we can remember long enough ago, we might envisage something like a speeded-up cine film, scene after scene rushing past as the projector whirrs. Now it is like browsing the internet at high speed, flicking from image to image in search of something, perhaps that vital bit of knowledge that will finally make sense of everything that has happened to us, and everything that we hope or fear may happen in the days to come.

... Up before daybreak, detecting a new softness in the wind and a hint of dawn above the hill, which say that spring is on the way at last...

... Standing in the rain, waiting for a bus that never seems to come...

... A long evening of wine and laughter with those who know us best but still love us most...

... Sitting in a consultant's office, sensing from the professionally downcast eyes that the latest round of treatment has not been successful...

... Walking on a deserted beach at the end of the day, as the waves break with barely a ripple on the sand and the sun grows huge in its sinking to the horizon...

… Quenched by misery as others look back to say with casual cruelty, 'We don't want you hanging round with us'…

… Curled in a warm and tender embrace on a sofa, as the television broadcasts something comfortably trivial…

… Waiting, with growing resignation, for a phone call that does not come, from those who have forgotten how much we used to matter to them…

Down, down, down.

As we descend, everything and everyone else is left behind —the good, the bad, the wonderful, the indifferent. Finally, we come to the very last step. We have arrived, but we have no idea where. The ground is slightly soft beneath our feet and the air smells faintly of damp earth. Cobwebs brush the head and cling to the face.

No sound, no light, no movement. Nothing to do for now, except wait in the silent darkness.

Now there was a good and righteous man named Joseph, who… came from the Jewish town of Arimathea, and he was waiting expectantly for the kingdom of God. This man went to Pilate and asked for the body of Jesus. Then he took it down, wrapped it in a linen cloth, and laid it in a rock-hewn tomb where no one had ever been laid. It was the day of Preparation, and the sabbath was beginning. The women who had come with him from Galilee followed, and they saw the tomb and how his body was laid. Then they returned, and prepared spices and ointments. On the sabbath they rested according to the commandment.

LUKE 23:50–56 (ABRIDGED)

This was the end, then. The beyond-nightmarish process of dying was finished, with each of the Gospel writers recording, for their own purposes, slightly varying versions of the events—what took place, in what order, and what words were gasped out by Jesus in his final hours. Perhaps the bleakest account is that of Mark. Like Matthew, Mark records no words of Jesus from the cross apart from the terrible cry of abandonment: 'My God, my God, why have you forsaken me?' (15:34). In contrast to Matthew's version, Mark only mentions the tearing of the temple curtain and the brief obituary offered by the centurion to indicate that anything special has occurred in the death of this homespun prophet from Galilee.

The possibility of being forsaken by God: that is the fear that we can trace through parts of the Old Testament because of the pervading knowledge that, again and again, God's people forsake him. It is one thing to choose to terminate or sit lightly to a relationship; it is quite another to be the one left forsaken by such a choice. Could God forget them? Would God forget them? The Psalms grapple with this fear with outspoken honesty and manage to return, in a matter of verses, to a state of confidence in God's enduring love and goodness. The exiles in Babylon were tormented by the knowledge that they had lost their homes, their temple, their land and their status, but the prophets reassured them that not only were they not forgotten by God, but that he would one day act to restore their fortunes.

The coming of Jesus, Emmanuel, should surely have established for all time the certain hope that God is with us, not against us or unmindful of us. It should have established that it is safe to believe in an eternal Presence, not an eternal

Absence—not even an everlasting Indifference. But in his cry of desolation from the cross, Jesus voices the appalling possibility of utter God-forsakenness. Some would argue that this was the moment when he was aware of carrying the sins of the world and was thus legitimately cut off from the Father, albeit for a brief spell. On the other hand, remembering that he was fully human as well as fully divine, might this not also have been the moment when, in his full and vulnerable humanity, he despaired? It had all gone wrong; he was going to die; there would be no last-minute rescue from the grave yawning before him. He had no choice but to fall into the dark.

God abandoned by God: there could be no worse betrayal.

This was the end, then.

Until you have seen it for yourself, it is hard to understand how absolute is the absence when the last breath has been taken, the heart has stopped beating, and the warmth of the life-blood has begun to dissipate. They have gone, leaving us behind, and we cannot follow. Picturing the scene at Golgotha, church tradition has given us the *Pietà*, the pitiful image of the Mother of God cradling the corpse of the Son of God, beyond consolation.

After any death, sooner or later, those left behind face the business of disposing of the body before it starts to decay. Perhaps in reparation for his refusal to save from execution one he recognised as innocent, Pilate released Jesus' body for a hurried interment in a pristine tomb. The women who loved Jesus prepared for a final intimate act of devotion, to anoint the body that, in life, could transmit the healing power of God at a touch.

The creeds tell us that after Jesus was buried, he descended to the dead. They did not know—those women, those men

—what the next line of the story would be: 'On the third day...' So they rested and waited for their work of mourning to continue. They rested not with the relief of completing a challenging task, but with the kind of total exhaustion that comes from having used up every scrap of emotional and physical energy. They were burned out, spent.

And here we wait too, in the silence, sightless in the darkness, empty in the emptiness.

Then we hear a voice.

We can't tell whether it is male or female, whether it is audible or speaking in the imagination of our hearts—but we can still hear it.

'What do you really want?'

What do we really want? What do any of us want?

Some of us want to party and, in the energy of the partying, to remake ourselves, become younger, glamorous, exciting, interesting, with a myriad futures still lying ahead of us.

Some of us want to achieve great things and, in the thrill of the achieving, to compensate for ourselves, become significant, recognised, influential, respected, changing the world so that everybody notices us.

Some of us want to be loved and, in the ecstasy of the loving, to forget ourselves, become secure, cherished, protected, held, never having to take a step or breathe a breath without the beloved cocooning us.

Some of us just don't know what it is; we simply know the hollow pain of the wanting...

And the voice says, 'Come.'

We step forward, moving blind, edging along a wall of rough, sweaty concrete towards the voice. At the very last minute, before we lose our final scrap of hope of a way out, the night around us starts to turn grey. Fresh, intensely cold air begins to flow from somewhere up ahead and all the while the light grows stronger and stronger.

## For reflection

'The last word of Christianity is not hell but victory over hell; God does not promise us universal salvation because he can only offer it to us and wait for our response, our love, to let it happen.'

OLIVIER CLÉMENT, *On Human Being*

Part Four

# The recovery of love

# 16
# The beginning

It is morning; walk with me.

In the growing light, look and see where we have come to, after that long descent through the cold and dark. We are standing in a walled garden. Red brick glows vivid in the early yellow sunshine, our breath rises in white clouds and there are touches of frost on the immaculate grass. Shrubs and trees wear their autumn colours and the luxuriant growth obscures the far end so that we can only guess at the size of this place.

Walk with me now, over the grass and towards the one who comes to meet us, his back to the eastern sky so that the dazzle of the rising sun obscures his face. He has come for our answer to his question—and, after all that, when you come down to it, the only possible response is so obvious, so straightforward.

What do we want?

We want to be made whole.

At the core of every heart, whether recognised or not, lies a longing for the one who made us, because, whether we know it or not, it is that one and that one alone whose love will set us on the path to recovery, whose love will bless us with the wholeness that we crave. The touch of that one alone can gift our crumpled, battered selves with balance, harmony and grace.

Our hearts can sense the pull of that foundational love and sense a longing to respond. When we come to the point of noticing this longing, beneath all other desires, we will have made a start along that path, on the only journey truly worth making. And the beauty and wonder of it is that the journey can begin before we even know the name of the one who is the end of our seeking.

As we journey, we will start to glimpse the beginnings of recovery, through love, of love—because until we are intentionally travelling towards wholeness, our ability to love and receive love will always be in some degree hampered by the many other hungers, fantasies and demands that force themselves on our attention, preening themselves as adequate substitutes for that foundational love. When we finally learn to see clearly, we will find that we begin to distinguish the satisfying from the hollow, the true from the false.

Look, see: he comes to us; his arms are held open in welcome and love. The invitation is for every one of us, here and now—to step into that warm embrace, to be held against the heartbeat of God, to drop the last tattered shreds of our resistance so that the healing oil of his gladness and blessing can flood us right through.

What it is to be so loved: to feel encircled by tenderness, held safe against every hurt, fear and nightmare. What it is to sense that presence in the sky above our head and in the ground beneath our feet, suffusing every created thing so that we realise at last how much the world brims with beauty, because we finally have eyes to see it. What it is to know that whatever else happens to us—and sadness and pain can and will come to us again because that is the way of this life— beyond, below, between and beside everything else, there is his love, inescapable, infinitely alluring.

There is time, now, to talk. We can walk with him, hand in hand, along the winding paths of this walled garden and we can tell him absolutely everything. We can talk on and on in the sure knowledge that there is no possibility of being misunderstood or judged unfairly or that he will grow bored and look over our shoulder for more interesting company. And when it hurts too much to go on, as it surely will if we are being truthful, he will hold us again until we feel strong enough to continue.

There is time—and more—to finish our story and then walk on together quietly. No need to say more or pester for analysis or answers, because we know that, for now, it is enough to have been heard; enough to be assured that our words have been received in love and the selves that we have shared so vulnerably will be cherished in love, without ending.

Here, we are safe.

Here, we have come home at last.

Now there was a woman who had been suffering from haemorrhages for twelve years; and though she had spent all she had on physicians, no one could cure her. She came up behind him and touched the fringe of his clothes, and immediately her haemorrhage stopped. Then Jesus asked, 'Who touched me?' When all denied it, Peter said, 'Master, the crowds surround you and press in on you.' But Jesus said, 'Someone touched me; for I noticed that power had gone out from me.' When the woman saw that she could not remain hidden, she came trembling; and falling down before him, she declared in the presence of all the people why she had touched him, and how she had been immediately healed. He said to her, 'Daughter, your faith has made you well; go in peace.'

Luke 8:43–48

It is painful even to imagine how desperate she must have been, to do what she did. This woman's condition meant that she was ritually unclean, contaminating until sundown everyone she brushed against so that they were obliged to go through a time-consuming cleansing process themselves. According to the Torah, a woman with irregular bleeding was unclean for as long as it lasted, and in this woman's case, that meant twelve lonely years. (Love-making? Hardly practical, and, anyway, it would contravene the purity code.) Twelve embarrassing, messy and financially draining years.

Day after day, week after week, month after month, year after year of drawing water and hopelessly washing, washing, washing over and over again. Besides that, she faced social and religious isolation, because those who were unclean were not allowed to enter the temple. Let us hope she had some friends who stayed close, defying the priests and the hygiene regulations and being willing to support her and pray with her that one day she would be well. Perhaps it was the love and concern of those hypothetical friends that gave her enough courage to venture out on that momentous day into the crowds around Jesus.

She would have been known, of course. Those of us reading this story in one of today's many anonymous urban contexts may struggle to understand how hard it is to go unnoticed and undiscussed in a small town or village. As she ventured out, she would surely have done so braced against disgusted looks and comments, as well as the sympathy that—while more welcome than hostility—would have eventually become cloying rather than comforting.

Nevertheless, she dared to go out and dared to go right against the strictures of the law, to defile the rabbi himself with her touch, in her desperation to be healed. Because he wouldn't know, would he? She simply had to reach out, and maybe, just maybe, it would be enough.

It was.

That wasn't all. What happens next is a part of the story that we may find puzzling. Why did Jesus not keep quiet and allow her to remain anonymous so that she could slip away in peace to treasure her healing? Why force her to disclose her presence so that she had to come 'trembling' and oblige those present to think about what must have happened to her? While we cannot presume to know his motives, it would have been clear to the crowd that by making public acknowledgment of her healing, Jesus was publicly putting an end to those twelve years of exclusion. He did so, moreover, using the tender word 'daughter', the only time in the whole of the Gospels that he is recorded as addressing somebody in this way.

The woman had to overcome not only her respect for her religious heritage but her fear and shame. At least she knew that she needed to be made well and, in her desperation, she was prepared to throw herself on the mercy of a stranger (albeit one with a growing reputation for miracles). Thus she found the healing for which she longed.

As we come to the point of admitting our own need, we must note that—as recorded in other miracle stories in the Gospels—the healing offered by Jesus also encompasses forgiveness of sins. Yes, we may bear unhealed wounds inflicted on us by others, but we should not try to blot out memories of what we ourselves have done. Yes, we may surely have been hurt, but, on reflection, we will soon realise that somewhere along the way we have also done cruel hurt to others, if only by lashing out in pain and fear, for self-protection.

In the loving, pervasive presence of the Lord God, we cannot hide from the fact that we are fully and completely known. Perhaps we show a calm face to the world, yet the nervous turmoil beneath our surface is known. Then again, we may present ourselves as sensitive souls, easily hurt, but the thread of steel that runs through our core is known, the steel that enables us to detach if necessary, and walk away, no matter how loud the cries for us to come back.

We are known, through and through, and, if we do not remember that, we may try to hide certain aspects of ourselves when it is utterly pointless to do so. At the same time, we must never, ever forget that we are known and yet we are still loved, eternally.

Look into the eyes of the one in whose presence we walk in the garden, and see that there is both love and forgiveness, gifts held out to us whether we are ready to take them or not. If we receive the gifts, we will find that they change us, and that may be a very painful process. But, as we have seen, being open to love involves being open to some kind of loss, if only loss of what was never worth keeping in the first place.

For now, let us be at rest, walking with the one whose arms are always open to hold us. We should not start worrying about how, when or where we will change or be changed, nor about how painful or costly that process may prove to be. If the context is love—and it is—our task is to set ourselves to learning that love, and learning what it means for us, for those among whom we live and work and try to love, and for the widest world beyond.

## For reflection

'The deep desire we hardly perceived breaks through the wants that we are able to see, and around which we made our conscious choice, and is immediately recognisable as the only thing we ever really wanted.'

PHILIP SHELDRAKE, *Befriending our Desires*

# 17
## Walking free

It is still morning but the sun is rising higher and the garden around us glows in the warmth and radiance.

Our walking has brought us along the paths, between the curtaining shrubs and trees, and finally to a wall at the bottom of the garden, covered with a climbing rose, which still bears a few late blooms, yellow and fragrant. Ahead of us is also a door, closed and bolted, and that is where our footsteps are taking us. Unlike the white door in the upper room that led us to the outside, this is a green garden door, perhaps the back door of this whole strange establishment.

Of course, there is no possibility of our leaving, by that or by any other way. To be quite clear about it, there is no foreseeable possibility of ever leaving, because this is where we have come home, where we have finally found safety. We know all too well what lies outside—been there, done that, and just about lived to tell the tale. There is no point whatsoever in even strolling past the exit.

'Actually, it is time to go on.' That voice, loving and gentle, and also authoritative past any gainsaying.

Impossible—we are absolutely far from ready to go anywhere else. We are too weak, too wounded and too afraid. If this is love (as we have assumed), how can love be telling us to go?

'Time for the next bit of the journey.' A hand, kind but firm on the shoulder.

Pleading is so embarrassing, but newly discovered love, apparently rebuffed, can force the heart and drive the mind a long way past worries about sounding undignified. 'What if goodbye is the last thing I feel ready to say? Isn't there so much more to talk about? Just a bit more time?' Panic tightens the vocal chords until the voice croaks.

'I didn't say anything about goodbye, but the journey is not a journey unless it continues, even if slowly. It is not a race. There is no ready or unready, just willingness to walk on and learn more as we walk.'

'What about those others?' More people have entered the garden from the house and we can glimpse them strolling about, alone or in twos and threes.

'It's not time for them yet—and don't worry, you can come back soon. You know the way here now.'

Are we willing to leave now, though? That is a hard question to answer when anxiety courses through us, when fear of what might come next—perhaps terror is not too strong a word for some—knots our insides. The worst of it is the threat of having to give up everything that we have just gained, in exchange for uncertainties that (our past experience shouts) will definitely not turn out to be for the better.

Willing or not, there is also the question of how we can be sure that we are strong enough. If life has broken us apart and we are newly remade by love, we are walking on wobbly limbs, working with the first little jolts of recently regained strength. The experience of healing may be as soft as the touch of early morning sunlight or as brutal as a stiff course of chemotherapy. If the latter, we are left feeling worse at the end than at the beginning, while knowing that it has been for the best (or so the experts have told us) and that we can start moving towards health again.

Assuming we have learned at least to recognise and name

our fears, the fear that waylays us at this point is the fear that we will find ourselves reverting to old patterns of behaviour, that old hungers will reawaken because they have not been properly sated. Very early one morning, or late one evening, or unexpectedly at the bright midpoint of the day, they will rise up again to dominate our waking hours and haunt our dreams. We worry that our beautiful wholeness, our healing, is just an illusion, a temporary feeling. Perhaps the safest outcome is to keep a few of those old options open, even if we know, deep inside, just how damaging they were. In our weakness and wobbliness, they can provide a bit of a crutch to help us limp along, well enough.

Fundamentally, we fear that our recovery—the recovery by and for love—cannot possibly last. The scars will break down. We will bleed once more, and, when we see the blood, we will fear that we have failed to change. And then we will be tempted back to despair.

> He was despised and rejected by others; a man of suffering and acquainted with infirmity; and as one from whom others hide their faces he was despised, and we held him of no account. Surely he has borne our infirmities and carried our diseases; yet we accounted him stricken, struck down by God, and afflicted. But he was wounded for our transgressions, crushed for our iniquities; upon him was the punishment that made us whole, and by his bruises we are healed.
> ISAIAH 53:3–5

These well-known verses come from the fourth and longest of a collection known as the Servant Songs in the second half of the book of Isaiah. Much quoted in the New Testament as a pattern for the gospel, they are generally assumed by most Bible readers to be a straightforward foretelling of the Messiah, Jesus. Like so many prophetic utterances, however, they are more mysterious than that.

The 'servant' has been identified as Israel, the nation chosen to show the world what it meant to be God's people. Then again, some have argued that the description of this figure was an oracle identifying a pagan king, Cyrus of Persia, who would be instrumental in God's purposes of eventually restoring his exiled people to their homeland. And then, in relation to the coming Messiah, many more have found that the Servant Songs provide a pattern for understanding who Jesus was and what he came to do, rather than simply presenting a precise forecast of events in the distant future.

However we personally choose to identify the servant, the poetry of these verses is a moving evocation of innocent suffering, endured to bring healing to those who are not even grateful, if indeed they have noticed what has been going on. Unjust suffering, the persecution of the innocent, will rouse most right-thinking people to indignation on behalf of the sufferers. If we find ourselves suffering in this way, it may be some small consolation for us to do so as martyrs, victimised for a righteous cause, fairly certain that posterity will vindicate our stance. Laying down our lives for our friends, too, is a biblically endorsed form of heroic behaviour that is clearly part of the way of loving and being loved.

It is quite another matter to be prepared to suffer for the ungrateful, the indifferent and the openly hostile, with no guarantee of a martyr's memorial.

We may read these verses too quickly, enjoying the sweep of the poetry and failing to summon up the mental images that the familiar phrases should convey. The 'servant' was somebody who was not just unpopular but whom people shunned, crossed the street to avoid. He was not just disregarded but was considered a byword for disaster, his misfortune so great that it generated horror rather than compassion. Yet this grotesque figure turns out to be a healer, despite (or because of) his wounded state, a sufferer whose grief inexplicably leads to recovery for the rest of us.

The English translation of verse 3 does not fully convey the fact that the word used for 'suffering' encompasses mental as well as physical trauma. It conveys the ache of broken bones and wince of lacerated skin but also the pain of the lacerated heart and ache of the broken spirit. This is one whose suffering is universal in scope, one who will, without a doubt, understand what we have felt or are still feeling.

This is the deep mystery: that this is not just a matter of empathy, a hand holding ours as we cry in the night. Somehow the wounding, crushing, punishing and bruising inflicted on the servant bring the hope of healing for our pain, frustration and brokenness. He has carried for us what we would otherwise find unbearable.

Who can explain how exactly this happens? There are no neat formulae to capture it, but what we do have in John's Gospel is the story of the risen Jesus, resurrection body still scarred, drawing Thomas to himself in love. Having willingly endured a horrific death and the grave, he walks again among his friends and followers, so imbued with power and grace because of what he has endured that his spirit changes them for ever.

Wounded and scarred, yet also healed and whole, he comes to us and invites us—the company of the wounded and scarred, yet healed and whole—to journey with him. As we do so, we will learn more of his love and learn that it is enough, if we know enough of it. This is surely one of the lessons that he longs to teach us, but we are so slow on the uptake. No matter what desires and hungers have harried us—this job, that lifestyle, those future possibilities, that wonderful person who will surely bring us happiness and fulfilment—the love that the risen Jesus teaches us can help us start to become complete in our own selves, just as we are, despite whatever we have done and whatever we have failed to do in the past.

Only then are we truly free to work, to serve, to play, and to love and be loved, not to top up our emptiness but because we are already secure in the everlasting love that desires our response so keenly.

We may be unsure whether we truly believe all this to be true as we approach the door in the wall, which he now holds open for us. We dare not look to see what lies ahead, and fear hobbles the feet, makes us reach out shamefully to clutch at the hand that points the way.

'You don't need to hold on. I am coming with you.'

What?

The alleyway through the door looks none too inviting and there is no clue as to where it will take us. That is the path before our feet, though. No other possibilities at present.

We go forward, but we do not go alone.

He is here too; his spirit is still with us.


### For reflection

'If the risen Lord did not still bear his wounds, then he would not have much to do with us now. The resurrection might promise us some future healing and eternal life, but it would leave us now alone in our present hurting. But because of Easter Day we already share in the victory. He still shares our wounds and we already share his victory of death. We too are now wounded and healed.'

Timothy Radcliffe, *What is the Point of Being a Christian?*

# 18
# Working together

We walk together along the alleyway, between high concrete walls that are tagged with graffiti in a rich variety of colours. Tread carefully: the sun glints off broken glass and the path testifies to the occasional presence of dogs and of people in various stages of intoxication. If we look back, hoping to glimpse an escape route, there is that hand again on our shoulder, that kind, firm hand, and the voice in our ear.

'This way.'

'Why?' It's a pathetic, bleating response, but surely we can't help it?

'Because there is so much more for you to know.' From the touch of that hand we feel a surge of electric energy, a burst of warmth and a sense of possibility. He is grinning at us. 'I tell you, don't worry. Everything will be all right, in the end. Come on, we're going this way.'

The alleyway turns sharp right and the high concrete walls are replaced by even higher brick ones. A single opening on the right-hand side leads to... wait a minute, we have come here before. The hidden, slightly ramshackle garden in the heart of the city, whose rose-beds are a little overgrown but still beautiful, where the compost heap has benefited from a recent deposit of grass clippings, and where the life-size crucifix stands and weeps behind the security fencing.

But we are not alone here, now.

There are other people in the garden—some kind of working party, by the looks of it. A couple of older women are weeding, a still older man is raking up a sprinkling of leaves to fill a wheelbarrow for the compost heap, and a couple of teenagers appear, from the state of their overalls, to have spent considerable time touching up the elaborate iron gates at the main entrance with fresh black paint. As we cautiously proceed, wary of these strangers (who are they? what exactly are they up to, and why?), one or two look up with a quick smile or wave of greeting. Others are single-minded in their busyness and purpose, undistracted even by new arrivals.

As we pause by the women weeding, we hear something of their conversation.

'You sound as if you're feeling better today.'

'Today has turned into a good day, yes. I didn't expect it, you know. When I opened my eyes this morning, my first thought was that I couldn't do it, couldn't face all those hours before I could go back to bed again. But what with one thing and another, it was OK, and now I am here and it is more than OK.'

'More than OK, definitely.'

They smile at one another and carry on working, side by side.

As we pass the leaf-raking man, he nods at us encouragingly. 'Go on, you're welcome to take a look around.'

We venture in a little further, and we see that the purpose and busyness has extended beyond the garden and even past the security fencing. This has been removed and propped against a tree, faded ribbons and washed-out cuddly toys still attached. Meanwhile, the crucifix itself lies flat against the flight of steps, which have been cleared of the toppling weeds and heaps of litter. Bent over the worn face, a middle-aged man is carefully applying what looks like varnish over renewed paint, which has brought the features back to vivid life. Pausing to stretch his cramped legs, the artist steps back and—perhaps because of the prone position of the crucified figure—our perspective shifts so that we see the wooden arms as not simply spreadeagled in agony but opened wide in invitation.

We also notice, for the first time, how the first two fingers of the right hand are extended in blessing, despite the nail driven through the palm. In the midst of mortal suffering, love is held out to us, for rejection or embrace.

'Almost finished.' The artist has noticed us watching him. 'It had a kind of beauty before, but in a sad way. Now, I hope, the energy and passion are easier to see, not just the brokenness.' He gestures round the garden at the clusters of people working away. 'Feel free to join in—there's plenty to do. You are welcome here.'

Beloved, let us love one another, because love is from God; everyone who loves is born of God and knows God. Whoever does not love does not know God, for God is love. God's love was revealed among us in this way: God sent his only Son into the world so that we might live through him. In this is love, not that we loved God but that he loved us and sent his Son to be the atoning sacrifice for our sins. Beloved, since God loved us so much, we also ought to love one another. No one has ever seen God; if we love one another, God lives in us, and his love is perfected in us.

1 JOHN 4:7–12

Far too many people laugh bleak, cynical laughs at the thought that the church could possibly be considered the embodiment of God's love. Right back at the beginning, early enough to feature in the New Testament, the Christ-followers were prone to disagreement, sharp fallings-out and grudging reconciliations. For some peculiar reason, the Almighty was persisting with his project of using frail and faulty human creatures to be the icon of his love for the rest of the world.

As the chosen people, Israel failed, fought, betrayed and generally turned their collective back on the One who had chosen them, so the church, the body of Christ, persistently underperforms (to say the least). Would most onlookers be quick to describe it as the visible community of the redeemed, a living embodiment of forgiving and transforming love, characterised by mercy, grace and a tireless passion to draw everyone into the light of God's kingdom?

Hardly.

Throughout scripture we can trace the pattern of human mess and chaos and divine forgiveness. When that forgiveness is acknowledged and accepted by those who have gone astray, healing and restoration can be released, and then the consequences of redemption, of that once-for-all atoning sacrifice, begin to be manifest. Each of us is a work in progress and so is the church, the corporate 'us', for God's love needs to be embodied in people-as-community as well as in individual lives. Each of us stands on our own in the heavenly presence; it is up to each one of us, on our own, to respond, or not, to the offer of love. In assenting to that offer, though, we find ourselves (like it or not) as part of a family, members of the Father's extended household. Just as in any human family, the family of God can be a distressingly uncomfortable place to be sometimes, but unlike any human family, this one will never, ever fall apart. Of course we can try to walk away from it, but the love that holds it together is inexhaustible.

The standard of God's perfection is inconceivably high

but the wonderful thing about it is that, unlike earthly perfectionism, it reveals our failings only in order to remedy them. The one who has begun the work of transformation in us will not be thwarted. His love, so we read in the passage above, is perfected in us.

Amazingly, then, we are—both individually and collectively —the icon of God's love, despite the fact that perfection remains a far-off dream. Like the first apostles after the resurrection, we are sent out to share the news of what we have heard and experienced long before we are ready, because there is no pass mark, no points system to designate A grade and B grade believers. There is a call to relationship, to making a journey into the heart of God. And if we take no more than the first step on that journey, if we say no more than a tentative 'yes' to that relationship, with the intention of walking on, learning and loving more, that is enough. We do not have to understand everything about a relationship or know the full details of the end of the journey before it can become a means of grace for us.

We are called to love, as we are loved, because that is how God's love is revealed. Fundamentally, the church is called to be the body that provokes the response, 'Can you believe how much they love each other?' In that love, however flawed it may be, we can nurture and encourage one another, living together and knowing that even when we come to the end, we need not fear dying alone. The love that we are learning, the love that is the oxygen of the heavenly kingdom, is not checked by a small matter like death.

The acknowledgment of this love and of the Son's redeeming sacrifice lies at the heart of the Eucharist, the meal of celebration, commemoration and commissioning that is the heart of the church's life. It is not a matter of sitting around and reminiscing about what happened more than 2000 years ago; it is not a matter of wrestling with the finer points of doctrine; we are simply called to re-enact, to taste, to see, to believe, and so receive a further measure of the healing fullness of God.

In the low-key, welcoming atmosphere in the hidden garden, it feels possible to stay and join in the work of tidying and beautifying. Nobody probes us with uncomfortable questions; most are generous with nods and smiles and unpressured guidance as to what to do where and when. The sun climbs to midday and the leaf-raking man produces sandwiches and crisps for everybody (enough for us too), and one of the teenagers returns from a corner shop with an interesting array of cans to share.

We sit down on the grass together, we eat, we drink, and we talk. All is well.

Is it perfect? No, of course it is not perfect. The sandwiches are a little dry, the cans of drink lurid in colour, and more than that, we can no longer glimpse the one with whom we came, although we sense his presence close at hand. Even so, in the sharing and conversation of this odd assortment of ordinary people, there is love, or at least the beginnings of love.

## For reflection

'I discover who I am, indeed become whom I am called to be, through interacting with my brethren and friends, discovering that they sometimes think that I can do more than I think that I can, but maybe sometimes less.'

TIMOTHY RADCLIFFE, *WHAT IS THE POINT OF BEING A CHRISTIAN?*

# 19
## Reaching out

The group's work in the hidden garden is done, for the moment. The crucifix has been replaced at the top of the steps, the newly delineated features bright with both pain and blessing. Before we leave, each person goes up to touch the feet of the figure, a gesture that is a kind of petition for all the others who will visit the garden in future. There is no question of replacing the security fencing to enforce distance. Instead, the two teenagers and the artist have fixed it to the stone wall and the women have planted honeysuckle and variegated ivy to grow between the wires and provide nesting opportunities for any small birds that find their way there.

We leave the garden, and, as the afternoon passes, we walk with the group through the streets, some of which we remember from our previous wanderings. Sometimes little tensions flare between two or three of the others and those of a more peaceful disposition have to intervene to re-orchestrate harmony.

'When we disagree more sharply,' says the artist, who has come to stroll alongside us, 'we have to stop everything and talk and talk—and sometimes just sit and be quiet with each other—until we have sorted it out. We've never yet got totally stuck. Perhaps that's because we've grown so close. I'm not sure…' He smiles and it's hard not to smile back, even though we question whether his words can really be true, given the history of the human race.

We are back in the heart of the city now, buffeted by the office workers hurrying to close the next deal or stopping dead as their mobile communication devices pester for attention. We skirt round the tense little knots of young men and boys who warily survey the surrounding streets for threats that only they can see. We wait at the traffic lights as a horde of 4 x 4s rush past, carrying children to carefully selected schools, windows tightly closed against the prevailing atmosphere. We wave over the fence at the off-duty lap-dancers relaxing with a smoke in the back yard of the local pub.

Somehow, walking together makes this place a little—just a little—easier to bear. Perhaps it will help us feel strong enough, secure enough, to start showing compassion to those we encounter in the relentless streets, instead of losing all sense of ourselves in a fog of fear and stress. Maybe that is why we have returned here, to learn to connect instead of wanting only to run away.

Then, suddenly, we are aware of the one who first found us and brought us back here. He is with us once more, guiding us away from the group, down a crooked little lane whose cobbles have amazingly survived every wave of decay, demolition and refurbishment. And at the end of this lane we can see the river, flowing fast in the direction of the far-off sea. Spanning the river is a footbridge.

We know we have no realistic choice except to follow him.

The bridge sways slightly as we make our way over, trying not to look down at the tidal currents that swirl rather too close beneath, carrying with them some of the city debris—planks of wood, plastic water bottles, a sandal, a thick mass of something white, disintegrating, unidentifiable.

Then we notice somebody waiting for us on the other side. Oh.

It would be so much less costly to connect with somebody

with whom we had no history, but this somebody is one we remember with uncomfortable clarity. Last time we saw them, they were leaving a cheerless flat, hand in hand with our rescuer; now they are almost (but not quite) unrecognisable because they are so shining with peace and joy. Can we possibly reconcile the damaged, damaging creature we remember with the shining somebody who stands before us now?

It would be so much less costly to ask forgiveness of those whom we have not hurt personally, from whom a negative response cannot do further harm to our hearts. We could confidently offer compassion and disinterested love if we felt fairly certain that it would be received with appropriate gratitude.

And then there is the strangest challenge of all: when the one we need to forgive, the one with whom we need reconciliation, is actually our own self, because towards ourselves we may be the most merciless of all.

The spirit of the Lord God is upon me, because the Lord has anointed me; he has sent me to bring good news to the oppressed, to bind up the broken-hearted, to proclaim liberty to the captives, and release to the prisoners; to proclaim the year of the Lord's favour, and the day of vengeance of our God; to comfort all who mourn; to provide for those who mourn in Zion—to give them a garland instead of ashes, the oil of gladness instead of mourning, the mantle of praise instead of a faint spirit. They will be called oaks of righteousness, the planting of the Lord, to display his glory. They shall build up the ancient ruins, they shall raise up the former devastations; they shall repair the ruined cities, the devastations of many generations.
Isaiah 61:1–4

As with so many of the Old Testament prophecies of consolation, the context here is harsh years of exile for God's people, lit up by an unshakeably confident hope of return and restoration. Everything will be changed. The Lord's messenger has been anointed to bring this good news to the bereaved, the ruined, the spent; and every image of brokenness is counterpointed with one of growth, life, celebration and freedom. Even the cities ruined for 'many generations' will be repaired: think of trampled fences, roofless dwellings that have been abandoned for as long as anyone can remember, and field systems that have turned into scrubland. Then, suddenly, long-lost descendants of the original inhabitants appear and enthusiastically set to the task of renewal and rebuilding their home.

Unless we have known some kind of personal exile, whether literal or figurative, it may be hard to grasp the full emotional force of hearing such words of promise for the first time. Maybe, though, we can bring to mind times when we have felt (or still feel) forgotten by God, abandoned on the scrapheap of life. Read the passage and notice that it is the ones who mourn who become 'oaks of righteousness', glorifying the gardener with their vigour and flourishing. It is these same mourning ones who are somehow transformed into the energetic city renovation workforce.

Luke's Gospel records Jesus reading out this passage in the synagogue at the start of his ministry and claiming for himself the role of the Lord's anointed—the literal meaning of 'Messiah'—to the growing consternation of the congregation, who knew him simply as Joseph's son. The messianic task was then entrusted to his disciples, to continue spreading the good news of God's kingdom to everyone who would listen.

And so the task comes down to us, to share the hope in our time and place, and also to allow the love of God and the Spirit of God to be visibly at work in us. Thankfully, the tide of love and grace is in no way dependent on our inadequate supplies of obedience or patience, or our extremely inadequate holiness. God is constantly reaching out through moments of grace, wherever and however, to connect with every one of his children. And God reaches past our most generous expectations to draw in those on the remotest margins, those whom we might very much rather exclude, not because they are 'unforgivable' but because they are just too angular to fit the space of what we prefer to define as 'church'—which, curiously enough, so often coincides with 'people like us'.

We should never, ever presume to set limits on his mercy; our calling is to stay focused on the task given to us and to everyone who has responded to Christ's call to follow: we must announce this good news and allow its consequences to be made visible in our homes, churches and communities. Thus we can pray that, over the course of our tiny lives, we may be permitted to serve as the means of enabling a handful of such moments of grace to happen.

Truth be told, it's strange how we persist in underestimating the sheer size and power of God, and persist in trying to erect flimsy tidal barrages against the eternal flow of love and grace. Unforgiveness, for example, can end up being more than a flimsy barrage. If we set about building unforgiveness into our lives, it's like planning the said barrage with the addition of a mean and precarious little house on the top, where we can retreat and nurse our grievances, well away from the world that has hurt us so badly. The tide will continue to flow and, although it will never destroy us, we will expend ridiculous amounts of energy resisting its force, shoring up the foundations of our retreat, clinging on to the bitterest of bitter ends to show how strong and competent we are.

We may develop self-justifying scripts to defend our position: 'I refuse to forgive because what was done to me was unforgivable... I refuse to be forgiven because I have done nothing that requires forgiveness... I refuse to be forgiven or to forgive myself because what I did was unforgivable.' Meanwhile, the other characters in our personal story may have let the tide carry them safely down to the sea, where they are enjoying a barbecue on the beach.

Of course there is a right time and there are appropriate places to offer and receive forgiveness, and we must seek wisdom to discern the rightness and appropriateness. Sometimes it is too soon and, sadly, it can sometimes be too late, in this life anyway. Standing, here and now, on the further bank of the river, the quaking of our hearts in fact confirms that it is indeed the right time to be brave enough to look into the eyes of the other.

It is the right time to step forward, the right time to unfold our defensive arms and humbly hold out our hands to them as they move towards us in peace and joy.

It is the right time, now, to exchange a holy kiss of peace.

All is well.

Such forgiveness and reconciliation may not unmake the consequences of what went wrong in the past, but it releases us to continue our own journey, a bit more whole and free than we were before.

When we look up, everything has changed.

## For reflection

'If we are serious in our commitment, then we can expect to be exposed to the probing, often disturbing Holy Spirit within, calling us to ever-deeper response. We will be challenged to trust more fully in the God who loves us too deeply to leave us within the supposed security of our limited horizons.'

BARBARA MOSSE, *ENCIRCLING THE CHRISTIAN YEAR*

# 20
## Dancing on water

Everything has changed.

The sun is sinking westwards, turning the river pure gold and flashing off innumerable city windows. In that astonishing light, it is as if we see more clearly than we have ever seen before, as if the glory of God has finally burst through the surface of things. Now we can see, too, that everywhere—above the river, perched on rooftops, poised on spindly spires and mobile phone masts, balancing along the gutters—there are the shining creatures that biblical convention calls angels, the messengers who go between the heavenly kingdom and the visible world.

Time has changed, too, kaleidoscoping between what has been, what is and what is to come. We look out over the city, and part of us is scared, because in this kaleidoscoping of time we see flames, faceless crowds surging through streets and squares, and we hear shouts of rage and despair and unanswered cries for help echoing from office block to office block. The smell of burning rubber stings the nostrils and a wind blows suddenly cold, sprinkling us with ash and oily smuts.

The city is finally consuming itself, but still the shining messengers rise and fall, converge and disperse, perhaps visible to nobody else but us, and now we can hear them singing. Their roaring anthem of praise tells us that, in the end, we do not have to fear, because the God whom they praise is mindful even of the most obscure corners of his creation.

Yes, everything has changed.

The one with whom we have exchanged forgiveness has gone. We are alone again, but the wonder of that encounter and the blessing of the shared embrace still encircle us in warmth. Standing by the river, watching the shining messengers, we sense within us no trace of the old, restless hunger and searching. Alone we may be, at the moment, but finally we know that we are complete as we are, in ourselves. Knowing that we are loved, body and soul, we can start to learn what it means to love as pure gift, rather than as anxious deposit given for the sole purpose of extracting a return.

Even as we treasure this new knowledge, the light starts to fade and, when we look up, we see massed cumulonimbus clouds rising to cover the sun. A storm is surely coming; the wind lashes our faces with rain and, in the gloom, for a heartbeat or two, we remember how it felt to be stalked by shadows, remember walking faster and faster to stay ahead of the fear.

What if…?

We dare not even frame the rest of the question, in case merely thinking the words makes the hunger real again, in case we wake from a dream of good to find that nothing has really changed.

'Don't be afraid.'

His voice—but where is he? Squinting through the rain, we scan the riverside to right and left, check out the bridge and even crane our necks to inspect the rooftops, but we can see no sign of him.

'Over here!'

There he is, as perhaps we should have guessed in the first place, standing in—no, on—mid-river, waving for us to come and join him.

Shall we?

But what if we go to him and he vanishes again before we are quite ready to be let go (as seems to be his way), and the river takes us under? What if this is the proverbial step too far, a ridiculously unreasonable demand after we have already done so much trusting and following?

Shall we?

His grin is irresistible.

Last minute to think: shoes off or shoes on? Check for keys, mobile phone, money. Better leave the coat behind, but what if we don't come this way again?

Who cares?

The river is still high, so the ladder down the embankment wall plunges straight into the water, leaving no safe strip of beach at the bottom for us to hover on nervously before taking the final decision.

So here goes.

Walking towards him on the glassy surface, we see nothing but his face and his outstretched hand, which grasps hold of ours and draws us to him. And as we dance together on the flowing tide, to the singing of the heavenly creatures, the sun breaks out from behind the storm and fills the sky with rainbows.

Then the angel showed me the river of the water of life, bright as crystal, flowing from the throne of God and of the Lamb through the middle of the street of the city. On either side of the river is the tree of life with its twelve kinds of fruit, producing its fruit each month; and the leaves of the tree are for the healing of the nations. Nothing accursed will be found there any more. But the throne of God and of the Lamb will be in it, and his servants will worship him; they will see his face, and his name will be on their foreheads. And there will be no more night; they need no light of lamp or sun, for the Lord God will be their light, and they will reign for ever and ever.

REVELATION 22:1–5

At the end we return to the words of the last book of the Bible, which gave us so graphic a picture of the godless city, Babylon, symbol of everything that sets itself against the kingdom of heaven. This time, we read again of the renewed Jerusalem, the healed and healing city, where we are promised that we will one day live, at home with God, for always.

Like all apocalyptic writing, the book of Revelation is concerned with revealing what is hidden, with presenting the true interpretation, the inside track, of otherwise baffling or terrifying events. Through its descriptions of giant locusts, fearsome horsemen, dragons, fiery lakes and general mayhem, the message is essentially simple: we know who is on the throne and whose finger is poised over the 'stop' button of history. God is sovereign; contrary to most appearances, his rule is the reality that lies about us, though hidden from our feeble gaze.

Here is the city as garden, a prospect more wonderful than the ancient wonder of the Hanging Gardens of the earthly Babylon, because the river of this new Jerusalem runs with the 'water of life', no less. In a dry land, water is never less than a precious resource but this river is akin to other rivers of heavenly quality found in scripture. It recalls the water flowing from the new temple to bless the restored land of Israel in Ezekiel's prophetic vision at the time of the exile, and an oracle of Zechariah that tells of 'living waters' (14:8) streaming from Jerusalem. It also recalls the river of Eden, described at the beginning of the story of God's dealings with the world.

As in Eden, and as in the vision of Ezekiel, so in Revelation the life-giving river is linked to trees of unearthly fertility. The passage tells of fruit crops every month, unimaginable bounty for those used to slaving and sweating to manage even two harvests a year. Even the leaves of this 'tree of life' bring healing, and where once a man and a woman were banished from a garden, lest they help themselves to the tree of life, now its healing goodness is offered to 'the nations'.

What is most wonderful about this new garden-in-a-city is that it is the setting for relationship. The purpose of the new Jerusalem is to be the throne room of God—and not only that, but also the place where, at long last, his people can see him face to face.

Face to face with God?

The whole of creation, you see, will finally and entirely be recovered in the love of God, re-covered with his love so that it will never again be naked and ashamed, suffering the blight of the original disobedience in Eden. Somehow, by the end of all things, we will have been made so pure and holy that we will be strong enough to bear the presence of the full majesty of heaven. We will not be cowering face down, shielding our eyes from the glare, but standing, face to face. We no longer need to fear separation, darkness, cruelty or pain, anything that might once have had the power to hurt the way we were individually created to be. There will be nothing to mar the beauty that is uniquely ours, that makes each one of us priceless.

This is the hope in which we live. This is the vision that tantalises just below the horizon of now. This is the city that will one day eclipse the shabby present reality of the Babylon world. This is the home towards which we are travelling but in which, at the same time, we already belong.

What exactly lies ahead for us? Sure, a heavenly destiny may await us in the end, but we cannot claim unerring foresight for tomorrow, let alone next week, month or year.

So what exactly does lie ahead for us? That is an unanswerable question, except in the most general terms, but one that still worries away at the peace of mind of so many, so much of the time. We want to know specifics, securities, to feel confident that our maps, our best-laid plans, every one of our hopes, dreams and desires, will fit into some grand scheme of life. We forget so readily that the road unfolds only as we walk it in trust and obedience. Our calling is to continue on the way, doing so in the knowledge that one day we will have God with us, face to face, always. There can be no greater hope; there is no greater promise.

Meanwhile, we can abandon ourselves to dancing on the golden, glassy river, safe in the hold of the one who saved us and will go on saving us for the sake of his tireless love. And as we dance, the river of light carries us on towards the ocean and the flaming west.

When, for now, the dance comes to an end, he releases us. Before we can do more, he is gone from our sight, his words still echoing in our ears.

'Follow me.'

What lies ahead? We cannot be sure exactly, but it will definitely be an adventure.

What will we find? There will be more companions along the way, more love, more friendship, more healing.

How do we know where to go?

Look for his footmarks.

Follow.

## For reflection

'Lot went to Joseph and said, "Abba, as far as I can, I keep a moderate rule, with a little fasting, and prayer, and meditation, and quiet: and as far as I can I try to cleanse my heart of evil thoughts. What else should I do?" Then the hermit stood up and spread out his hands to heaven, and his fingers shone like ten flames of fire, and he said, "If you will, you can become all flame."'

FROM *THE DESERT FATHERS*, TRANSLATED BY BENEDICTA WARD

# Author's note

In the writing of *The Recovery of Love*, I have found a number of other books to be particularly inspiring, some of which I have quoted. I list them here for interest and as suggestions for further reading, if you like.

Hans Urs von Balthasar, *Prayer,* (Ignatius Press, 1986)

Olivier Clément, *On Human Being,* (New City, 2000)

Andrew Clitherow, *Desire, Love and the Rule of St Benedict* (SPCK, 2008)

David Eagleman, *Sum* (Canongate, 2009)

Andrew Jones, *Pilgrimage* (BRF, 2011)

Belden Lane, *The Solace of Fierce Landscapes* (OUP, 1998)

John O'Donohue, *Anam Cara* (Bantam Books, 1997)

John O'Donohue, *Eternal Echoes* (Bantam Books, 1998)

Timothy Radcliffe, *What is the Point of Being a Christian?* (Burns & Oates, 2005)

Timothy Radcliffe, *Why Go to Church?* (Continuum, 2008)

Philip Sheldrake, *Befriending our Desires* (DLT, 2001)

# Sources

Epigraph: Rachel Boulding, from *New Daylight*, 27 September 2010 (BRF).

## Part One: In search of love

Planet Babylon: Margaret Silf, from *New Daylight*, 1 October 2011 (BRF).

Constant craving: Damon Galgut, *In a Strange Room* (Atlantic Books, 2010), p. 106.

Broken: Belden Lane, *The Solace of Fierce Landscapes* (OUP, 1998), p. 35.

The hidden garden: Timothy Radcliffe, *Why Go to Church?* (Continuum, 2008), p. 18.

Found: Christopher Cocksworth and Rosalind Brown, *Being a Priest Today* (Canterbury Press, 2006), p. 193.

## Part Two: Because he first loved us

He chose her: Andrew Clitherow, *Desire, Love and the Rule of St Benedict* (SPCK, 2008), p. 5.

He cherished her: Clitherow, *Desire, Love and the Rule of St Benedict*, p. 125.

She cheated on him: John O'Donohue, *Anam Cara* (Bantam Press, 1997), pp. 89–90.

She enraged him: Hans Urs von Balthasar, *Prayer* (Ignatius Press, 1986), pp. 224–225.

But still he loves: Teresa Morgan, *Seasons of the Spirit* (BRF, 2010), p. 59.

## Part Three: Love and loss

The mother: love: Teresa Morgan, *Seasons of the Spirit* (BRF, 2010), p. 47.

The friends: love: Timothy Radcliffe, *What is the Point of Being a Christian?* (Burns & Oates, 2005), p. 105.

The friends: loss: A.M. Allchin, *The Joy of All Creation* (DLT, 1984), p. 144.

The mother: loss: Allchin, *The Joy of All Creation*, p. 146.

The end: Olivier Clément, *On Human Being* (New City, 2000), p. 153.

## Part Four: The recovery of love

The beginning: Philip Sheldrake, *Befriending our Desires* (DLT, new edition 2001), p. 63.

Walking free: Timothy Radcliffe, *What is the Point of Being a Christian?* (Burns & Oates, 2005), p. 75.

Working together: Radcliffe, *What is the Point of Being a Christian?*, p. 139.

Reaching out: Barbara Mosse, *Encircling the Christian Year* (BRF, 2012), pp. 145–146.

Dancing on water: Benedicta Ward (trans.), *The Desert Fathers* (Penguin, 2003), p. 131.

Also by Naomi Starkey

# Pilgrims to the Manger

## Interactive Bible meditations

This book is an invitation to a pilgrimage through Advent, to Christmas itself and on to Epiphany. As the days and weeks pass, we will reflect on a range of issues—the significance of the festivities, the values that underpin our lives, some of the other special days in the Church calendar at this time, and how we can begin to deepen our understanding of God's perspective on our world, our church and ourselves.

'Pilgrimage' is more than a figure of speech in this book, however. You are invited to join an imaginary group of pilgrims on a path that starts in an average high street and leads through and beyond the city, offering lessons from the sights and sounds encountered along the way. It's not a conventional pilgrimage, following a well-trodden route to a well-known destination, but it is a pilgrimage of both head and heart that will help us to explore something of what it means to say that God is with us. We will see, too, how this truth brings both challenge and consolation for us as we follow the Christ-child.

*ISBN 978 1 84101 709 9    £7.99*
*Available from your local Christian bookshop or, in case of difficulty, direct from BRF: please visit www.brfonline.org.uk.*

# Walking with Gospel Women

## Interactive Bible meditations

## Fiona Stratta

Imaginative meditation can be a powerful way of attuning ourselves to God's presence, involving as it does the emotions as well as the mind. This book offers a refreshing and inspiring way into Bible study, using meditative monologues based around many of the women of the Gospels. Through a time of guided reflection, we identify with the woman concerned and see what lessons emerge for today as we ponder her story.

Each chapter consists of a monologue, linked Bible passage and discussion material designed to draw out deep communication and group fellowship, as well as transformational learning. While designed primarily for small groups meeting to grow their relationships with God and with each other, the monologues can also be used as a way into silent reflection either for individuals or with larger groups.

*ISBN 978 0 85746 010 3    £7.99*
*Available from your local Christian bookshop or, in case of difficulty, direct from BRF: please visit www.brfonline.org.uk.*

*Also available for Kindle*

# Dreaming of Home

## Homecoming as a model for renewal and mission

## Michael Mitton

Finding a sense of 'home', a special place of acceptance and belonging, is a fundamental human longing. In this powerful and profound book, Michael Mitton shows how it is, in fact, an essential part of both personal development and spiritual renewal. Drawing on his own experience of the 'homecoming' journey, he considers how we can go about finding our true home within God's eternal kingdom, how to identify the forces within us that may hinder this search, and the importance of churches offering a welcoming home to all.

Each chapter concludes with questions for personal reflection or group discussion and the book also features an imaginative retelling of the parable of the prodigal son, addressing some of the issues raised through a story-based approach.

*ISBN 978 1 84101 877 5*    *£7.99*
*Available from your local Christian bookshop or, in case of difficulty, direct from BRF: please visit www.brfonline.org.uk.*

*Also available for Kindle*

# Pilgrimage

## The journey to remembering our story

## Andrew Jones

The age-old practice of pilgrimage is more popular than it has been for centuries. At a time when the Church seems increasingly exiled and estranged from our culture, more and more people are treading the ancient pilgrim routes, whether they are committed Christians, spiritual seekers or simply curious. The renewal of faith that they find on their journey often outweighs what happens in many churches.

Andrew Jones shows how pilgrimage can awaken those at all stages of belief to remembering the story of God's creating and redeeming work in history, which tells us who we are, where we have come from and where we are going. The act of remembering it not only offers a life-transforming way out of exile but points to the way home, to the place where we can live authentic and balanced lives. The book concludes with a focus on eight popular places of pilgrimage in the British Isles, drawing lessons from their history and spiritual heritage that can encourage and inspire us on our own faith journeys.

*ISBN 978 1 84101 834 8   £8.99*
*Available from your local Christian bookshop or direct from BRF: visit www.brfonline.org.uk*

# Rhythms of Grace

## Finding intimacy with God in a busy life

# Tony Horsfall

*Rhythms of Grace* emerges from a personal exploration of contemplative spirituality. Coming from an evangelical and charismatic background, Tony Horsfall felt an increasing desire to know God more deeply. At the same time, he felt an increasing dissatisfaction with his own spiritual life, as well as concern at the number of highly qualified and gifted people involved in Christian ministry who experience burn-out.

In this book he shows how contemplative spirituality, with its emphasis on realising our identity as God's beloved children and on being rather than doing, has vital lessons for us about discovering intimacy with God. It also provides essential insights about building a ministry that is both enjoyable and sustainable.

*ISBN 978 1 84101 842 3   £7.99*
*Available from your local Christian bookshop or direct from BRF: visit www.brfonline.org.uk*

*Also available for Kindle.*

# Writing the Icon of the Heart

## In silence beholding

# Maggie Ross

In *Writing the Icon of the Heart*, we are invited to share the reflections of one who, over the years, has spent long hours in silence and prayer in one of the world's most wild and solitary landscapes, as well as the more urban context of Oxford. Casting new and often startling light on ancient texts and long-established spiritual practices, Maggie Ross shows how faith cannot be divorced from an outlook characterised by a rigorous questioning and testing of assumptions, and a passionate concern for the created world in which we are blessed to live.

*ISBN 978 1 84101 878 2    £6.99*
*Available from your local Christian bookshop or, in case of difficulty, direct from BRF: please visit www.brfonline.org.uk.*

*'Maggie Ross invites us into real quiet, which is also real presence, presence to ourselves and to the threefold mystery that eludes our concepts and even our ordinary ideas of "experience". A really transformative book.' (Archbishop Rowan Williams)*

# When You Pray

## Daily Bible reflections for Lent and Easter on the Lord's Prayer

# Joanna Collicutt

In these Bible readings for Lent and Easter, Joanna Collicutt shows how growing as a Christian is rooted in the prayer Jesus gave us. As we pray the Lord's Prayer, we express our relationship with God, absorb gospel values and are also motivated to live them out. As we pray to the Father, in union with the Son, through the power of the Spirit, so we begin to take on the character of Christ.

The Holy Week readings encourage us to pause, watch and wait at this special season; commentary is kept to a minimum and we spend time reflecting, in the light of the Lord's Prayer, on Luke's description of Christ's passion and resurrection.

*ISBN 978 0 85746 089 9   £7.99*
*Available from your local Christian bookshop or, in case of difficulty, direct from BRF: please visit www.brfonline.org.uk.*

*Also available for Kindle.*

# Enjoyed
## this book?

**Write a review**—we'd love to hear what you think.
Email: reviews@brf.org.uk

**Keep up to date**—receive details of our new books as they happen.
Sign up for email news and select your interest groups at:
www.brfonline.org.uk/findoutmore/

### Follow us on Twitter @brfonline

**By post**—to receive new title information by post (UK only), complete
the form below and post to: BRF Mailing Lists, 15 The Chambers, Vineyard,
Abingdon, Oxfordshire, OX14 3FE

| **Your Details** |
| --- |
| Name _____ |
| Address_____ |
| _____ |
| Town/City _____ Post Code _____ |
| Email_____ |

| **Your Interest Groups** (*Please tick as appropriate) | |
| --- | --- |
| ☐ Advent/Lent | ☐ Messy Church |
| ☐ Bible Reading & Study | ☐ Pastoral |
| ☐ Children's Books | ☐ Prayer & Spirituality |
| ☐ Discipleship | ☐ Resources for Children's Church |
| ☐ Leadership | ☐ Resources for Schools |

### Support your local bookshop
Ask about their new title information schemes.